Intersections

Readings in Sociology

General Editors

Ralph B. McNeal, Jr.
University of Connecticut

Kathleen A. Tiemann
University of North Dakota

A Customized Sociology Reader
Compiled by:

Prof. Jennifer A Robinson

Family Law

C123

University of California, Irvine

Criminology, Law and Society

PEARSON

Custom
Publishing

Director of Database Publishing: Michael Payne
Sponsoring Editor: Robin J. Lazrus
Development Editor: Catherine O'Keefe
Editorial Assistant: Ana Díaz-Caneja
Marketing Manager: Kathleen Kourian
Operations Manager: Eric M. Kenney
Production Project Manager: Marianne C. Groth
Database Project Specialist: Elizabeth MacKenzie-Lamb
Rights Editor: Francesca Marcantonio
Cover Designer: Renée Sartell

Cover Art: "Apartments in Buenos Aires, Argentina," by Glen Allison, courtesy of PhotoDisc. "Figures," courtesy of Eugenie Lewalski Berg.

Printed in the United States of America

Please visit our website at *www.pearsoncustom.com*
Attention bookstores: For permission to return any unsold stock, contact Pearson Custom Publishing at 1-800-777-6872.

ISBN: 0536119279

PEARSON CUSTOM PUBLISHING
75 Arlington St., Suite 300
Boston, MA 02116

Preface

The fascination of sociology lies in the fact that its perspectives make us see in a new light the very world in which we have lived all our lives...

Peter Berger

Pearson Custom Publishing and General Editors Ralph B. McNeal, Jr. and Kathleen A. Tiemann are proud to bring you *Intersections: Readings in Sociology.*

Our highest goal in the creation of *Intersections* is that it does, in fact, assist you in capturing that 'fascination of sociology' Peter Berger refers to above and which so many of us, as teachers, want to impart on our students. A traditional way of doing this has been to expose the students to central sociological ideas and examples of sociology in action through a book of readings. While *Intersections* is a reader, it is anything but traditional due to the way it is being provided to you.

With *Intersections*, we have endeavored to provide you with a rich and diverse archive of high quality readings in such a way that both professors and students will have easy and cost-effective access to the minds and ideas that illuminate and help explain some of the central ideas and issues of sociology. Within *Intersections* you will find over 380 readings and 19 topical introductions—both of which will be updated and expanded on a regular basis—from which you can choose only those readings and introductions that are germane to your particular course. No longer will you and your students have to be dependent on the standard large and expensive 'one-size-fits-all' college reader, which often includes more material than will be covered in the course, yet often also lacks those particular pieces that are viewed as essential by individual instructors. In addition, a classification system for each selection provides helpful information on how the selections might be organized to allow the various perspectives on the course to be pursued. Although the primary course for which *Intersections* was developed is the introductory sociology course, the size and quality of the database may also make it a good resource for a variety of other courses such as marriage and family and gender studies.

However it is used, it is our ultimate hope that you will find *Intersections* to be an essential source of readings in sociology—a source noted for its depth, breadth, and flexibility—that meets the highest scholarly and pedagogical standards.

Acknowledgements

A project of this scope cannot be undertaken without the assistance and advice of our colleagues. We wish to thank the following people who helped us tremendously in the development of *Intersections*.

Andrew Scott Ziner (Cedar Crest College) wrote introductions for two sections: "Aging" and "Health & Medicine"; Charles M. Brown (Ohio University) wrote introductions for the "Religion" section; David A. Merrill (University of Wisconsin) wrote introductions for both "Politics & the Military" and the "Work & the Economy" section; and, lastly, Donald Branson (University of Connecticut)

iii

wrote an introduction for our readings on the environment ("Population, Communities and the Environment.")

In addition, the project idea and execution was reviewed several times as it was being developed, and each of the following provided valuable feedback and suggestions which strengthened the project: Victor Agadjanian, *Arizona State University*; Kathleen Almquist, *Mesa Community College*; Robert Althauser, *Indiana University*; Andrea Baker, *Ohio University of Lancaster*; Felix M. Berardo, *University of Florida*; Dennis F. Berg, *California State University, Fullerton*; Karen Bourg, *Nashville State Community College*; David L. Brunsma, *University of Alabama, Huntsville*; Russ Buenteo, *University of South Florida*; Thomas Calhoun, *University of Nebraska*; Allison R. Camelot, *California State University, Fullerton*; Lori Campbell, *Ohio State University and Ohio Wesleyan University*; Ralph Cherry, *Purdue University, Calumet*; Ione Y. DeOllos, *Ball State University*; Michael Dreiling, *University of Oregon*; Gregory Elliott, *Brown University*; Morten G. Ender, *United States Military Academy*; Polly A. Fassinger, *Concordia College*; Charles Faupel, *Auburn University*; Celestino Fernandez, *University of Arizona*; Theresa J. Fish, *Lake Superior College;* Lisa Frehill, *New Mexico State University*; Robert Futrell, *University of Nevada, Las Vegas*; Susan G. Greenwood, *University of Maine*; James Hawdon, *Clemson University*; Laura Hecht, *California State University, Bakersfield*; Shirley A. Hill, *University of Kansas*; Amy Holzgang, *Cerritos College;* Robert B. Lee, *Foothill College*; Diane Levy, *University of North Carolina, Wilmington*; Michael Lewis, *Christopher Newport University;* Philip Luck, *Georgia State University*; Kristy McNamara, *Furman University*; Phyllis Myers, *Normandale Community College*; Carrie Uihlein Nilles, *Marshall University*; Milagros Peña, *University of Florida*; Brea L. Perry, *Indiana University;* Karl Pfeiffer, *University of Alaska*; Mary F. Radosh, *Western Illinois University*; Terry Reuther, *Anoka-Ramsey Community College*; John Reynolds, *Florida State University*; Randi Rosenblum, *Hunter College*; Michael T. Ryan, *Dodge City Community College;* Constance L. Shehan, *University of Florida*; Jim Spickard, *University of Redlands*; Sue Spivey, *James Madison University*; John Stolte, *Northern Illinois University*; Peter Taylor, *Colorado State University*; Celeste Watkins, *Northwestern University*; L. Susan Williams, *Kansas State University*; R. Dean Wright, *Drake University*; Mary Lou Wylie, *James Madison University*; Andrew Scott Ziner, *Cedar Crest College*.

SOCIOLOGY READERS FROM PEARSON CUSTOM PUBLISHING

Create the reader that matches **your** syllabus!

Effective pedagogical apparatus - headnotes, end-of-selection questions, and optional introductions included with all selections!

Intersections: Readings in Sociology
www.intersectionsreader.com

An archive of 380 of the best classic and contemporary readings in sociology. Readings not only elucidate the discipline, but also help spark student interest in the entire area through the richness, diversity, and breadth of its readings. Select only the content you wish to use in your course to reflect your teaching methods and course perspective.

Inequalities: Readings in Diversity and Social Life
www.inequalitiesreader.com

The most comprehensive collection of high-quality readings on multiple forms of inequality and how they intersect. More than 175 classic and contemporary articles reflect theoretical, conceptual, and global perspectives to match the goals and objectives of your sociology or interdisciplinary –oriented course.

Crossroads: Readings in Social Problems
www.crossroadsreader.com

An essential source of over 300 essays and readings that illuminate and help explain central ideas and issues in the study of social problems. Choose from a rich and diverse archive of high quality articles that cover topics and present perspectives germane to your course.

Boundaries: Readings in Deviance, Crime and Criminal Justice
www.boundariesreader.com

More than 350 classic and contemporary readings that cover all the topics addressed in deviance, criminology and criminal justice courses. The richness of this repository of readings provides unlimited flexibility and timely solutions to create a reader that fits your course and teaching style.

Reading Women's Lives: The Customizable Reader for Women's Studies
www.readingwomenslives.com

Nearly 500 selections are available including literature, pieces that reflect multicultural and cross-cultural diversity, readings drawn from the social sciences and third-wave feminism readings. Nineteen optional thematic introductions to key topics in Women's Studies – themes such as The Body, Difference and Inequality, Feminism and the Women's Movement, Sexualities, and Socialization.

www.pearsoncustom.com/sociology

Contents

v

Recreating Motherhood

BARBARA KATZ ROTHMAN
Baruch College and the Graduate Center
of the City University of New York

In this reading, Barbara Katz Rothman argues that we need a new way to think about "mothering." She further contends that changes are needed to properly support the rights and needs of mothers. All told, Rothman advocates a total "recreating" of the concept of motherhood.

The ideology of capitalism, that goods are produced for profit, is clear to us; we know that some societies avoid the profit motive, and that most societies feel there should be some limit on the extent to which human life is viewed as a commodity. It may seem farfetched to apply this ideology to motherhood and to children. But the family has always been an economic unit as well as a social and psychological unit. What is new, perhaps, is the shift from children as workers to children as commodities, accompanying the change in the family as a unit of production to its new role as a unit of consumption.

For the most part, children aren't workers in the family anymore. The farm family in rural, traditional American society is mostly a thing of the past. Because children don't become real partners in work, they become, in a sense, luxury items. We talk about children in very much the same way we talk about other luxuries: Can we afford a second car? Can we afford a third child? Accompanying this change in the way we see children is a change in our view of motherhood. No longer an event shaped by religion and family, having a baby has become a part of a high-tech medical world. There is artifi-

"Recreating Motherhood," by Barbara Katz Rothman, reprinted from *New Perspectives Quarterly*, Vol. 7, 1990, pp. 53–57.

cial insemination, amniocentesis, contract surrogacy; during labor, a doctor manages the process, making it more efficient, predictable, rational. Likewise, when mothers and fathers push their babies onto a schedule, so that feeding the baby meshes into the nine-to-five day, parenting becomes an exercise in the rational and efficient use of time.

And this, I fear, is where it is all heading: the commodification of children and the proletarianization of motherhood. We are no longer talking about mothers and babies at all—we are talking about laborers and their products.

❂ Mind-Body Dualism

Ours is a liberal philosophical tradition which holds that what is especially valuable, about human beings is the capacity for rationality. But hand in hand with the valuing of rationality is a theoretical disdain for the significance of the body, and a disdain for physical work in preference of "mental" work. The later, dividing the physical from the mental work, and then using machines and people interchangeably to do the menial physical work, is the essence of technological organization.

Blue-collar work is less valued than managerial work. The "white collar" is a status symbol for having risen above the work of the body. This division of labor is a particular problem for women as mothers: mothers *do* the physical work of the body, women *do* the menial work of body maintenance. Thus women become identified with the physical, the body, and men with the higher, the rational.

This mind-body dualism has deeper consequences as well: by viewing the body as a mechanism of production, we are encouraged to see it as a resource to be used. If the mind and rationality are held "above" the body, it becomes relatively easy to see the body as a resource for the use of the mind, and, specifically, women's reproductive bodies as "societal" resources. And it is here—between the body as "private property" and the body as "resource"—that we encounter the ubiquitous problem of reconciling individual freedom and social order.

❂ The Body as Private Property

In the U.S., legal recognition of the body goes only to the view of it as individually owned. That is an idea deeply rooted in our liberal political system and our economic system, which is based on private ownership and free enterprise. And it is not a bad way of *legally* viewing the body: as property, privately and individually owned. Such a view protects each of us from all of us; protects us as individuals from potential abuses of power by the government.

In fact, intelligent feminist use of this individualist ethos has been invaluable in assuring women's rights in procreation. Once women are recognized as full citizens, then individual women must be accorded the same rights of bodily autonomy and integrity afforded men. For women, that means sexual and procreative autonomy. Because it is her body, she cannot be raped. Because it is her body, she cannot be forced to bear pregnancies she does not want. Because it is her body, she cannot be forced to abort pregnancies she does want.

Due in part to our current battles over the right to abortion, we tend to think that the three branches of government "permit" women to have abortions; as if the drive for continuing pregnancies came from the government, and the drive for abortions from women. In fact, the legal protection works also to permit women not to have abortions. When women's ownership rights over their bodies are lost, the rights to have and the rights *not* to have abortions are likewise lost.

In American society, when we bring it back to the simple legal question—who can force an abortion or forcibly prevent one—we wisely retreat to safety, calling forth our most sacred value: the power of ownership.

This then is the way women have successfully been able to combine America's liberal philosophy with its economic ideology. Women have made use of the mind-body dualism, to allow a view of the body as owned, like a shelter which houses the more important mind. If one claims rationality for women—the essential liberal claim for all people—then simple fairness gives women the same rights of bodily ownership that men have, and the very high value of ownership, of property rights, is then turned to the advantage of women who can claim exclusive rights to their own bodies. In the name of ownership, women have demanded access to contraception, sterilization, and abortion.

Yet, while the "owned-body" principle has worked for women in avoiding motherhood, it is less clear how it can be made to work to empower women as mothers. A woman's body may be her own, but the bodies of mothers are not highly valued. In fact, in pregnancy women may simply be seen to own the space in which the fetuses are housed. This is the argument on which attempts to control women's behavior during pregnancy are based: owning her own body is not enough to assure her civil liberties if her body is believed to contain potential wards of the state. The anti-drug, anti-drinking "behave yourself" campaigns aimed increasingly at pregnant women, along with the judicial trend toward prosecuting drug-abusing mothers for "transporting illegal drugs to a minor" through her umbilical cord, are the most blatant examples of this trend toward separating the rights of the women from the rights of the fetus growing in her womb.

Is it possible to make the legal concept of the owned body work in the interest of mothers? Women could take advantage of mechanistic thinking, and claim "sweat equity" in their babies: they are ours because we have done the work to make them. Women would then have made the connection between the owned body and the owned child. But the "sweat equity" idea will work only if women's labor, the "sweat," is valued.

❂ The Limitations of Liberal Feminism

Though a great deal of progress has been made by the women's movement, as it stands, a generation of women have grown up to be exactly the kinds of parents they wanted their children's fathers to be. Women earn good money at secure, responsible, interesting jobs. Women take their work seriously—but they balance it against the needs of family.

With a few glorious exceptions, men have not taken up the slack. While women have added full-time employment to the traditional mother role, men have mostly just added a few hours, at best, of "quality" time to traditional fathering.

The feminism that spread with the Industrial Revolution and that wanted to give women "equality with men" was liberal feminism, the feminist thinking that dominated the first, and probably the current, wave of the women's movement.

The simplest and least threatening version of feminism is to ask for what is seen in American as simple fairness. Demands for fairness consist largely of the insistence that prevailing liberal ideals be applied to women: equal pay for equal work, the same rights for women as for men, etc. Since in America we are living in a society founded on liberal principles, liberal feminism comes closest to mainstream values.

Liberal feminism has its roots deep in American culture; feminists as far back as Abigail Adams requested that the framers of the Constitution "remember the ladies." Liberal feminists, in asking that the ladies be remembered, were not so much offering a critique of American life and values as they were seeking full access.

Liberal feminism works best to defend women's rights to be like men, to enter into men's worlds, to work at men's jobs for men's pay, to have the rights and privileges of men. But what of our rights to be women? The liberal argument, the fairness argument, the equal rights argument, these all begin to break down when we look at women who are, or are becoming, mothers. Pregnancy is like nothing else, so how can uniqueness be made to fit into an equality model?

Liberal feminists, seeking equality and recognition of women's rationality, but discounting the value of the woman's body, claim equality of parenthood between men and women. It is, after all, only women's bodily experience that is different from men's.

Liberal feminism does not challenge the mind-body dualism posited by and embedded in liberal philosophy, and so falters. Liberal feminism has no place for the inherent physicality of gestation and lactation, and no respect for the "menial" work of body maintenance: the mothering work of early childhood.

"Equal rights" sound good. But a focus on *rights* ignores *needs*. Giving women all the rights of men will not accomplish a whole lot for women facing the demands of pregnancy, birth, and lactation. Because of the focus on formal equality, because of the value of mind over body, and because of the manner in which our technologically-oriented society seeks efficiency through the separation of work and home, physical and mental, etc., liberal thinking tends to diminish the significance of the physical parts of motherhood.

As individuals, separation and compartmentalization form a central theme of liberal society. We "change hats"; "shift gears"; we carry our separate selves around, experiencing not only the compartmentalization between people, but within ourselves as well. We have "work lives" and "home lives." We change clothing in our different roles, we change style, we change tone.

Yet against this, we have motherhood, the physical embodiment of connectedness. We have in every pregnant woman the living proof that individuals do not enter the world as autonomous, atomistic, isolated beings, but begin socially, begin connected. And we have in every pregnant woman a walking contradiction of the segmentation of our lives: pregnancy does not permit it. In pregnancy the private self, the sexual, familiar self, announces itself wherever the woman goes.

Motherhood is the embodied challenge to a liberal philosophy which serves to articulate the values and themes of technological society: order, predictability, rationality, control, rationalization of life, the systematizing and control of things and people as things, the reduction of all to component parts, and ultimately the vision of everything, including ourselves, as resources.

For those people who want to see women—their bodies, sexuality, motherhood—treated with respect, liberal feminism fails.

☙ The Atomization of Life

Though liberal feminism has fallen short in many respects, the idea that "the personal is political" was an early insight, a shining, glorious insight of the women's movement. These women understood that the celebration of the individual's power to create, to overcome, etc. fell very hard on the people who were structurally placed so as not to be able to achieve.

Individualism is a deep-rooted theme in American society. Yet, because we as a society have conceptualized everything in terms of the individual—that it just takes gumption, strength, initiative—we must continually deal with the failure of the individual. We have obscured the structural barriers to success behind infinite examples of individual failures.

As long as we keep asking how working mothers can resolve their problems, the terms "working" and "mother" will remain an inherent contradiction.

The question should be: What is wrong with the way we have organized family and work so that they don't fit together? Certainly, two major social institutions should match. If they don't, there is a problem. And if we have created a notion of "work" in occupation and profession that precludes women from living full lives, there is something wrong with the social and economic organization of "livelihood."

First and foremost, we must rethink the nature of the family, and gender relations within the family. At the absolute height of the feminine mystique, for instance—when every mother was supposed to be in her home, in her own kitchen, with her own children—breast feeding in America was at its absolute low point. Regardless of biology, American women were standing over the stove sterilizing formula for their babies. So, one could not even claim that the mother needed to be at home to breast feed her baby.

Pregnancy, on the other hand, is certainly biological. But the issue of pregnancy, and the six-week maternity leave, has never really occupied the center of the family/work debate. The issue does not revolve around the physical experiences of pregnancy or birth. Rather, the issue centers on the care of children and the organization of family.

The nucleus of the debate is the three-month old that cannot be abandoned on a hook; it is the three-year old that needs attention; it is the six-year old that comes home from school at 3:30, though work ends for his parents at 5:30.

Women may not need fathers to share the mothering with, but they certainly need someone. Women cannot do it all. The problem of the double day for women, the unending circuit of paid work, and then work in the household, not enough sleep, and back to work, inevitably takes its toll.

The fact is that the social relationship of parenting, of nurturing and of caring, needs a social base, not a genetic one. Through their pregnancies, women begin to establish that base. But if women are not to drop from exhaustion and lose all pleasure in life, someone is going to have to help with the kids.

Mothers are working in the nexus between the child and society. Children need their lives preserved and their growth fostered. The social group needs that growth shaped in ways appropriate and acceptable to it, for its own continuation, preservation and growth.

Maternal practice must meet three interests then; those of preservation, growth, and acceptability. The initial and most powerful demand is preservation: simply keeping the child alive, especially through its vulnerable early months and years, beginning, for birth mothers, with conception. But the mother must do more than keep this heart beating: she must foster the child's physical, emotional, and intellectual growth. And she must do that in such a way that her child becomes an acceptable adult. Both for the sake of the child and for the sake of the society of which the mother, too, is a member, the child must fit in, must grow to meet the needs of the society.

Looking at motherhood this way, as a discipline, a way of thinking, a response to the needs and demands that exist outside of the mother, shifts our focus from who the mother is to what she is doing. Who she is, who she feels herself to be, is deeply gender based: she is a woman, a mother. What she is doing is not gender based: the similarities in behavior of mothers has more to do with the similarities in their situations, in the demands they face from their children and from their societies, than it has to do with similarities in the women. And so the person engaged in this discipline of motherhood need not be a mother, need not be a woman, in order to engage in these activities, this way of thought and practice that is mothering.

Perhaps this is one of those moments of crisis a society faces, where there are two paths that can be taken. We can focus on nurturance, caring, human relations. We can come to accept and to respect a wider variety of family relationships and arrangements. Those qualities we have come to think of as maternal could become more widely shared, by both men and women. We could direct this nurturance, this maternal caring, not just to children, but to each other. The values and the experience of motherhood could come to shape the way we live in the world. This is, I suppose, the fantasy, the truly revolutionary potential of a recreated motherhood.

Or we can recreate motherhood to reflect the commodification of children and the degradation of the mothering project. That, I am afraid, is the direction we have been heading in for a long time, and what we are faced with now is the *reductio ad absurdum** of this process.

A society that creates a decent environment for motherhood is a civil society. It is a world that is supportive of nurturance, of caring, of involvement with one another.

---

* Eds. Note–Disproof of a position by showing the absurdity to which it leads when taken to its logical conclusion.

◉ ◉ ◉

Questions

1. How has our conception of children changed over time? Why has it changed?

2. Rothman says that "for those people who want to see women— their bodies, sexuality, motherhood—treated with respect, liberal feminism fails." What does she mean?

3. According to Rothman, how should we think about motherhood? Why should we look at it this way?

4. How do you think about motherhood? Do you agree or disagree with Rothman's position? Explain your answer.

After Divorce: Investigations into Father Absence

TERRY ARENDELL
University of Wisconsin–Madison

Why do some men become absentee fathers after they divorce? Terry Arendell's interviews with divorced men reveal that absence is a technique that some men use to actively manage the stress that they feel after a divorce. This article explores divorced men's attitudes toward fathers' rights and their obligations to their children.

This article specifically investigates the phenomenon of postdivorce paternal absence using data obtained through intensive interviews with 75 divorced men (Arendell, forthcoming). All respondents in this exploratory study were residents of New York State, had one or more minor children, and had been divorced or legally separated for at least 18 months. . . .

Shared generally by these divorced fathers were definitions of their postdivorce situations, explanatory frameworks, and perceived lines of action. Specifically, a large majority of the fathers routinely discussed the phenomenon of father absence in similar ways: as being a direct consequence of men's experiences with women and divorce. Even most fathers who continued to be involved with their children perceived absence to be a viable option not only for other men but also

"After Divorce: Investigations into Father Absence," by Terry Arendell, reprinted from *Gender and Society*, Vol. 6, No. 4, December 1992. Copyright © by Sociologists for Women in Society. pp. 562–586.

11

for themselves under certain, conceivable circumstances. Differences in marital or visitation status, whether married or not or involved with their children or not, did not account for the discursive, or programmatic, similarities and variations within this group. Nor did custody status dictate or negate participation in the dominant discourse.

One of the central themes of the masculinist discourse of divorce was the notion of *rights*. Framed as issues of rights and having a direct relationship to father absence were changes in relations of power and authority; such changes included not only adjustments made but losses perceived. Actions taken primarily in response to feelings experienced were also defined as matters of rights.

☺ Absence as a Strategy of Action

A strategy of action is a persistent way of ordering action through time (Swidler, 1986). The objective of postdivorce absence as a strategy of action is the avoidance or circumvention of further conflicts, tensions, and certain emotional states and uncertainties. It involves three interrelated and overlapping components: actual practice, a perceived or optional line of actions, and emotion management.

A Practice and Optional Line of Action

The boundary between absence as a practice and absence as an optional line of action is ambiguous and problematic: the point at which the option became practice for the fathers in the study was not always discrete and identifiable since absence often came about as a result of omission rather than commission. That is, absence was not always a deliberate decision taken at a particular point but often became a condition over time as the gaps between contacts or visits with the children were allowed to lengthen. Further, certain fathers perceived their relations with their children to be so tenuous as to make the possibility of becoming a fully absent parent realistic.

Postdivorce absence as a practice and an option was, specifically, a strategy of action aimed at controlling particular situations. Primarily to be controlled was interpersonal conflict with the former wife and, occasionally, with the children of the ended marriage.[1] With the exception of the small number of fathers characterized as androgynous, the vast majority were engaged, or had been until their withdrawal from their children's lives, in highly antagonistic relations with their former wives. These conflicts, for the most part, were a continuation of the character of the marital relationship, at least as it unraveled. Dissension between the former spouses often involved issues of contention carried over from the marriage and the specifics of the divorce property settlement. But most conflict was centered on their children who constituted the primary postdivorce link between them. Conflicts over children were complex: not only did specific issues evoke disagreement but the former partners often viewed child-related matters from distinctive positions and in divergent ways. One noncustodial father, for example, told of a continuing quarrel with his former wife.

> I gave my son a shotgun for his 12th birthday and she had a fit. She was afraid he was suicidal, he was so depressed over the divorce, his failing grades in school, and our fighting. She was sure I was giving him the message it was okay for him to shoot himself. I viewed the gun as a symbol to him that I trusted him, that I had confidence in him to pull through all of this. I was right too: he never did hurt himself and he seems normal now [at sixteen]: he likes to hang out with his buddies and drink beer and he likes girls. I understand what it is to be a boy growing up; she doesn't. It's important for him to learn to be a man and he can't do that without my input. But she'd like to see me completely out of their lives.

Concerns and disagreements about children's well-being were often based on some form or another of evidence and were sometimes grave. Parents intent on using whatever was available to them in their ongoing interpersonal struggles, however, could deliberately exaggerate or fabricate concerns regarding their children who were both readily available and relatively powerless pawns in the postdivorce hostilities. The specifics of disagreements over children varied, centering generally on issues related to their living arrangements, care, treatment, and economic support. Mothers and fathers accused each other of neglecting their children including, for example, leaving them alone without supervision or sending them to school or to the other parent's home in dirty and torn clothing. In a unique twist, one custodial father accused his former wife of neglect for leaving their child with him rather than assuming primary custody as he believed mothers should. Quarrels over children's educational experiences and moral and religious guidance were common. Allegations of physical and sexual abuse were exchanged between the former spouses and, according to the fathers, were disproportionately attributed to them. Ten fathers had been formally investigated on the basis of such allegations.[2]

Postdivorce conflicts, although not universal, were common experiences among the men participating in the study regardless of their level of discontent with the divorce outcome. Contributing to conflicts was the defining of family relationships within the context of rights. As a constitutive element of the shared masculinist discourse of divorce, rights had a distinctive connotation: generally, *rights* was used with that which was expected, desired, and believed to be deserved as a *man*. The rhetoric of rights, widely available in the culture at large and appropriated from political and legal theory and practice, encompassed beliefs about individualism, autonomy, choice, control, and authority, beliefs that are also central to the cultural conventions and norms of masculinity (Jaggar, 1983; Pateman, 1990). Rights as used by these divorced men with regard to their family situations and experiences then was a euphemism for male privilege within the stratified gender system. Especially at issue were the privileges of position and roles of husband and father as held in the family prior to separation and divorce. Thus framed in the language of rights were matters of control and authority in the postdivorce family including, given the dominant legal rules that formally place minor children into parental custody after divorce, questions of access to children. Moreover, the securing of rights was perceived to involve fundamental issues of identity itself: protecting an identity as a masculine self required preserving, or seeking to preserve, sundry spheres of dominance and control (Arendell, forthcoming). Men satisfied with their divorce and postdivorce experiences spoke of rights in ways analogous to those men who were intensely dissatisfied with nearly every aspect of their divorce experiences. The principal exceptions were those fathers characterized as androgynous.

The securing of one's rights was a formidable and continuing enterprise sometimes involving the legal system and typically involving struggles with the estranged spouse: the actions of former wives were often characterized in various ways as "intended to deny me my rights." The primary use of rights entailed a highly personalized contest or competition, involving a polarized outcome of either winning or losing. That rights were to be secured in relationship to another (even if oppositional) demystified the assertions and implications that what was at issue were matters of abstract principles of justice. For example, in discussing his postdivorce experience, a father who had opposed the divorce and subsequently withdrawn from the lives of his five children, recalled,

> When the judge gave my house to my wife [who was living with and caring for the children], he took away my right to manhood. He took it away and left me with nothing. He stripped me clean.

Losing the family home represented for this father the various losses brought about by the divorce; the family home is to many men "a cultural symbol of power and success" (Riessman, 1990, 152). Various other fathers explicitly observed that the legal system "had emasculated" them by revoking their rights to control their earnings and ordering them to pay child support. Some men talked of having to fight for their "rights to their parenthood."

The rhetoric of rights fostered an objectifying of relationships and an emphasis on fathering as an achieved status rather than a particular complex of interactional processes and dynamics. Children were often discussed specifically in the context and terms of rights, especially *father's rights;* they were defined as a kind of property over which control was to be contested and fought. Contemporary legal dictates and procedures reinforce the stance that children are objects to be fought over by divorcing parents (Emery, 1988; Weitzman, 1985) although "father right," as traditionally institutionalized in the law, has undergone considerable challenge and change (Polikoff, 1983).

Among the fathers using the language of rights to discuss actions taken with regard to their children was this noncustodial father who had his child "snatched from his mother" (his words) by having him taken from a school playground in another state and put on an airplane to New York. He described has efforts and the judicial decision made after 18 months of court hearings and delays:

> My "child snatching" was a huge success. It was a big score. But the judge upheld my ex-wife's custody by ruling that my son was "too young" to be with me. Besides, I didn't really want custody. My son was a kid and needed his mother, I knew that. And I wanted my freedom. But it was all-out divorce war. It was just like an A-bomb: I wanted my son for awhile and got back at her, all in one fell swoop. I legally stole him, just simply resorted to *child snatching*. I'd never really wanted custody. I just needed to flex my *rights*. After all, I still was his father; I wanted to have some say in his life. I needed for him to know that I still had some control around here.

He continued, reflecting on his subsequent withdrawal from his child's life:

> I finally decided that I was putting too much energy into this divorce-war with my ex-wife. We'd played this game for over four years. So I pulled out; she didn't even know when to say "uncle." Someday, if my son wants to get to know me, he can find me.

The entanglement of questions of access to and authority over his child with antagonisms toward and power struggles with his former wife was common among the participants in the study. So too was this father's use of rights as an explanation for aggressive and confrontational actions. Although his tactics were more extreme than most described, eight other fathers reported having engaged in some form of child abduction activities, giving similar explanations for their efforts.

The condition of being a "visiting father," as the noncustodial parent referred to themselves drawing from both legal and popular terminologies, involved extensive interpersonal conflict and emotional turmoil and served as a basis for postdivorce paternal absence.[3] Visitation was an issue of particular significance to the father without sole or co-custody because it is the legally defined and protected means of access to one's children after marital dissolution (Novinson, 1983). Despite its institutionalization as a parental arrangement, visitation, both as a concept and practice, was engulfed in ambiguity and was a source of extensive dissatisfaction and, for some fathers, particular outrage. Rejecting the status assigned to them in the postdivorce situation as that of visiting father, several withdrew totally from their children's lives. One man characterized his absence as "a response to the condition of 'forced impotence,' a response to the total denial of my rights." Another person, who became an absent father after unsuccessful attempts to obtain shared custody, said,

> I will not be a visiting uncle. I refuse to let some woman [my former wife], judge, attorney, or social worker reduce me to that status. I'm a parent and parents do not "visit" their children. If I see my child only every other weekend, I become nothing more than a visiting uncle. I am a father in name only at this point. Until and unless I can be a father in every sense, I simply refuse to have any part of this. If someone came and stole my child from my house window, there'd be 500 volunteers combing the area. When a wife steals a child, "well, go about your work and if you're really good you'll get ever other weekend." These are the things I face, the philoso-

phies that men face. Our rights as fathers are simply negated, erased.

This father's further comments point also to the understanding expressed in numerous ways by these men that the family is predicated on marriage. In this definition of family, relations with children are entwined with those with the former wife and so, likewise, can be transitory.

> Besides, you know, every time I see those children, I am overwhelmed by memories. They are a living reminder of *my* marriage, *my* wife, and the years of pointless effort. Being a father is all tied up with being a husband. That's ended.

Visitation, or the activities and logistics of being a visiting father, typically entailed power struggles between the former spouses; in turn, strategies and tactics aimed at obtaining control usually involved visitation in some way. Most fathers, including those who were involved with their children at relatively high levels, insisted that their former wives had hindered their access to their children. Some fathers encountered persistent interference: scheduled visits were denied, telephone conversations interrupted or prevented, messages not conveyed, and mail intercepted and not given to the child to whom it was sent. The "cat and mouse game," as several fathers described it—going to pick up their children for a visit and finding no one home—was an experience described by nearly half of the fathers and was a recurring one for some. As this father of three recounted:

> Every time I went to pick them up, they'd be gone. I'd drive all the way [40 miles from his residence] over there, as we'd agreed and after I'd called her the night before to remind her, and they'd all be gone, every one of them. Even the neighbors were in cahoots with her; they'd insist they hadn't seen any of them the whole day.

Such actions led some men to initiate court hearings to protest and prohibit the interference. Others, including several who believed that the utility of court proceedings had been exhausted, began to allow longer periods of time to lapse between contacts and visits. Indeed, over half of the fathers fully absent from their children's lives became nonvisiting ones over an extended period of time and after a series of confrontations with the former wife.

Failures both of communication processes and imagined alternative lines of action added to the postdivorce interpersonal quagmire. Two absent fathers, for example, noted that they would like to reestablish contact with their children but did not know how to do so. One asked,

> How do I explain to them my absence from them? How do I explain that even though I gave up, I still am their father? I have a difficult time rationalizing that myself.

If visitation was the issue that former wives could use as the tactic of ultimate provocation in the postdivorce hostilities, as alleged by a majority of the fathers, then initiating a challenge to maternal custody was the comparable strategy available to them. Dissension and discord could be continuously played out by challenging or merely threatening to challenge maternal custody status. (Three fathers had fought to obtain custody *during* the divorcing process and had obtained custody; these men like the other three who became sole custodial parent without a custody fight at the time of divorce, were raising their children as single fathers.) More than three-quarters of the fathers without primary custody from the time of separation indicated that they had threatened their former wife with a custody fight since the divorce agreement had become final; more than a quarter had gone through an attorney to make a formal threat. Predominantly at issue in custody challenges, as with the phenomenon of father absence generally, was the relationship with the former spouse and not with the children, and this relationship was fundamentally about issues of power and control. For example, in discussing the problematic relationship between himself and his former wife, this man stated,

I always know that whenever things get too out of control I can threaten her with a custody challenge. So far, and I've spent over twenty-five thousand dollars, I've lost. But the point is that she and I both know that I can slap a suit against her anytime I want to. She's on the defensive. Economically it kills her. I can make it up in a few good months but she's on a fixed salary.

Another father, discussing his repeated use of custody challenges as a response to his outrage over visitation interference, accounted for his lack of success in changing the custody situation by arguing that a legal bias that overwhelmingly favors women prevails. The belief that mothers are unjustly privileged in custody matters was prevalent among these men, even those who were satisfied with their own situations.

After that particularly nasty fight over visitation, I took her to court again. I got the usual crap from the judge: "that it's just awful that you fight this way and that you should be ashamed." Judges always look at me when they say that; their eyes are on me. I think what they mean is that "you are the only one here who has rationality, you should be stopping this. Also, you're male so you're inherently wrong, that's why I'm looking at you." And he refused to change the custody, even though he agreed with me that I was correct and she was wrong; he told her not to do it again. Judges would never let men get by with these violations, but women get by with murder in these cases.

Only three fathers had successfully obtained a formal change in child custody and each had subsequently returned the children to their mothers. Two of the three men had then joined the ranks of absent fathers, claiming that they were weary of fighting with the former wife. The primary objective of their court actions had been to torment their former spouses, not to obtain daily parental responsibility for their children.

That a formal custody challenge was sometimes used to harass a former spouse did not exclude other objectives although it did tend to taint them. Several fathers who had lost their custody challenges, including two who had subsequent cases pending, sought custody changes because they believed their children's safety while in their mothers' care was at risk. Confounding their legal cases, however, was the fact that each of these men had been involved previously in extensive and public interpersonal conflict with the former wife; consequently, court personnel viewed these fathers' actions with suspicion and questioned their motives.

Child support was another especially volatile and meaningful issue, and anger about it was standard. Noncompliance with court orders mandating support was not limited to absent fathers, although they had proportionately much higher rates of nonpayment; only one absent father was contributing to the financial maintenance of his children.[4] Refusing to pay child support was described as a legitimate response to unfair treatment from both the legal system and the former wife and was an action typically defined in terms of violated rights. Paying irregularly or not at all was explained also as a way to punish the former wife for various actions and attitudes. Conflict, noncompliance with child support agreements, and father absence were related: the under- or nonpayment of support were ongoing subjects of disagreement contributing to the move to a state of absence. In turn, absence was used to justify nonpayment. One absent father, who was vehement in his rejection of the role assigned to him as a visiting father, explained his refusal to pay child support:

> Why should I have to pay for children who[m] I do not live with and who[m] I do not have a part in raising? By paying child support, I simply reinforce my ex for having left the marriage and denied me my children. What kind of logic is that? Why should I have to add to my losses by paying out my hard-earned money? So I take my chances that they'll [the legal authorities] throw me in jail. But I refuse to pay.

Alluding to the ambiguity regarding father-child relationships and parental activities and responsibilities in the postdivorce situation, several absent fathers noted that their children were living with stepfathers who, because they "had the pleasure of living with them," should be responsible for their support. For them, since divorce terminated any direct parental involvement, the obligation to provide economic support was ended, as this father suggested:

> Not only would I be paying money to her so that she could then spend it on herself, and not the kids, but she has a husband who can afford to support them all. He lives with them; he can support them. We are no longer a family. Why should I support *that* family?

Nearly two-thirds of the men who paid child support regularly expressed an understanding for fathers who refuse to pay support. That child support payments involved a one-directional transfer to the former wife, who was not required to be accountable for its use, was uniformly vexing and viewed as a violation of their rights to control their earnings and have independent lives. Moreover, being obligated by law to provide funds regularly to the former wife was symbolic, representing a shift in the balance of power between them. Child support was defined as constituting "unearned gifts" or "largess" to their former wives rather than as contributions to the support of children. One father described former wives generally as "leeches seeking to drain men dry." Another claimed that "child support taught children, and particularly girls, a welfare mentality in that it tells them that men will always pay their way." Several men insisted that they simply refused to be "money machines" for either their ex-wife or their children.

These divorced men complained that fathers are recognized within the legal system primarily or only as income providers. As evidence, they pointed to the disregard of expenditures made for items other than child support as well as to the restrictions imposed on their access to their children. Expenses incurred while their children were with them, such as those for food, entertainment, and travel, were not recognized by the courts in their cases. Nor was money spent on gifts or clothing acknowledged even when such items were needed by the children; judges dismissed such spending as "voluntary" and not relevant to the discussion of child support levels or payment compliance.

Another issue that infuriated the men was the link made by former wives between child support and visitation. Former wives tried to justify their interference with visitation by leveling charges of inadequate child support payment, although the two are legally defined as distinctive issues. Claims regarding child support were used to harass them in other ways as well. For example, explaining the experiences leading to his absence, this father stated,

> She kept insisting that I was hiding money, that I had lied to the judge by filing a false income statement. She knew I was unemployed and that I was only behind in making support payments because I didn't have a cent. Yet she announced that "if you don't pay, you don't get the kids." The fact that I had lost my job was totally meaningless to her. Actually, she believed I quit the job on purpose so that I wouldn't have to pay support. That's what she kept telling her attorney and my kids.

While they complained about the amount of support ordered, arguing that it would have been even higher had they not actively resisted the former wife's demands and her lawyer's efforts, only three fathers indicated that their own financial status was hampered seriously by the support ordered, and two of these fathers were unemployed. All fathers interviewed, however, described men who were impoverished by child support payments. Widespread among these fathers was the belief that financial hardships by divorced men are common but are glossed over in the media and by researchers while those experienced by women are exaggerated. One man characterized the media coverage of the economic outcomes of divorce as "feminist propaganda intended to discredit men."

Largely absent from these fathers' accounts was the scope of their own or other men's participation in the constructing and maintaining of high levels of postdivorce conflict. Tactics and lines of action, such as insistence on achieving a particular outcome, intimidation, and aggressiveness, and seeking to exert control rather than to locate areas for compromise, were defined as necessary responses to particular conditions rather than interactional constructions to which they were party.

Emotion Management

As a strategy of action, absence was used also as a means of emotion management (Hochschild, 1983). That is, absence, served as a strategy for handling the various and powerful emotions integral to their postdivorce experiences. Emotion management served "to sustain a certain gendered ego ideal" (Hochschild, 1990, 24) or to reinforce self-identity. By managing their feelings and directing them along certain avenues, these men empowered themselves in their assertions that they "remained in control," both of themselves and their situations, despite the unfamiliar, complicated, and usually emotionally stressful postdivorce circumstances. Through absence, fathers could distance themselves from the reminders of earlier experiences and limit involvement in situations likely to elicit particular feelings. The avoidance of their children or former wives, or the regular issuing of threats to become absent, were not the only emotion management strategies taken by these men. Other reported actions included drinking excessively; using drugs, particularly cocaine; self-imposed social isolation or, at the other extreme, excessive levels of social activity including the seeking out of a number of women for casual relationships; overt conflicts with friends and other family members; and greatly increased involvement with work. Engaging in any or many of these actions did not exclude also using or threatening to use absence.

Pivotal in many postdivorce conflicts were intense feelings regarding the former wife; anger toward her was a particularly common emotion. Thus absence was often used or considered as a means to preclude further angry and hostile interactions with the former spouse. Absence was also used to limit physical violence: nearly half of the men in the study reported incidents in which they had resorted to violence or had threatened it with serious intent since separating from their wives. "She drove me to it" was a common refrain among the men describing the use of force. Many of those recounting violent episodes insisted that their former wives had "set them up," usually by violating their rights in some deliberate way, seeking to incite violent behavior to justify limiting their access to their children. But even as the men attributed responsibility for their use of force to the former wife, they also acknowledged its efficacy for them. The threat or use of physical force served as a means to reassert control in the immediate situation, to release pent-up feelings of frustration and anger, and to terminate or avoid the search for other problem-solving strategies. The dynamics of interactional violence tended to overshadow all other issues between the man and woman.

Moreover, hostile and aggressive acts also served as a defensive posture against other, usually less familiar or acceptable, feelings. Anger itself was a form of emotion management, and anger, if not already felt, could be triggered readily by defining issues as violated rights. Other feelings, such as sadness and sorrow, loss and pain, and fear, could sometimes be disregarded, denied, or left unexamined by being defined as facets of anger. Anger could be identified, expressed, and directed in ways that other emotions could not be, especially given most men's limited experience in dealing with other divorce-related feelings, such as distress and sorrow. As Riessman (1990) notes, "Men's various manifestations of distress have one thing in common: the distancing of self from feelings of sadness" (p. 153); men "have trained incapacities in the language of feelings . . . they take their distress into the realm of action" (p. 159).

Although given far less attention by the men in their accounts, other emotions contributed to the phenomenon of postdivorce absence and were intertwined with feelings of anger. Unresolved and intense feelings of loss about the ended marriage and the former partner, for example, played a significant part in several men's motives toward ceasing involvement with their children. One father indicated that it was the emotional turmoil prompted by his former wife's remarriage that finally pulled him totally away from his children: "Her marriage was the final nail in the coffin." Another indicated that he saw his children rarely because he had "only finally begun to heal" from the loss of his wife and the end of his marriage. "Seeing my children simply reopens old wounds. It's better to avoid the reminders of the past."

In contrast, several fathers attributed their limited, declining, or total lack of involvement with their children to a gamut of emotions pertaining directly to them. One father, unusual among the participants in the degree to which he distinguished his feelings from those of anger, discovered that relating to his son sporadically rather than routinely during daily family life prompted unbearable feelings of sorrow and loss. He described this experience:

> Every time I pulled up to the driveway to let him off, it was like part of me was dying all over again. I could barely keep myself together long enough to give him a hug goodbye; I knew it wasn't good for him to leave seeing me so visibly upset each time. He would open the door, step out of the car, and I would feel as if I would never see him again. He would walk up to the sidewalk and a sense of grief would utterly overcome me. It would take me several days to pull myself together enough to even function at work. I'd have to keep his bedroom door closed; I couldn't bear to see his empty room. I had to break it off totally just to survive; the visits themselves were terrible because I had this constant unease, knowing what was coming.

Other fathers also found the contacts with their children to be intensely discomforting, though in varying ways. Numerous fathers found themselves confronted with a kind of on-the-job training for which few guidelines were available. Fathers were neither familiar with negotiating the parent-child relationship independent of the children's mother nor were they prepared for the changes prompted by divorce. The ambiguity surrounding what it meant to be a divorced father was only exacerbated by these fathers' feelings of anxiety and sense of uncertainty, particularly during the crucial early months following the marital separation when children looked to their parents for guidance in the altered situation. One father, alluding to the disruption of his former role as the authority figure in the family said,

> I found that I really couldn't control my boys except by getting angry. They just argued and fought when they were around. Every visit was incredibly tense; we were like coiled rattlesnakes just waiting to strike. I'd end up losing my temper which just made it worse because they treated me like I had no right to punish them.

Most fathers either did not try to establish a routine of family life or were unable to achieve it when their children were with them. The time together was defined as a "visit." Fathers sought primarily to entertain their children, continuing former family recreational activities or exploring new ones together. Only two fathers enjoyed this approach, one of whom noted,

> We [my two sons and I] played really well together so it works out great. We have a terrific time together. We're like kids together.

While representative in its reference to the awkwardness of visits, the following excerpt is unique in the extent to which the father explicitly expressed empathy for his six-year-old daughter's experience:

> How many times in one day, after all, can I take my daughter to McDonald's or to the park to swing? I just don't know what to do to entertain her. So we end up renting videos and spending hours just sitting in front of the TV screen.

I am restless and bored. She is unhappy although she tries, she really does seem to try. She needs to be out playing with her friends, not stuck here with me.

Having been divorced about 18 months, this father continued to be involved with his child but indicated that his contacts with her had been declining steadily over the past year; at the time of the interview, he had neither seen nor talked to her for nearly four weeks. He avoided telephoning her because her anticipated that she would inquire about his plans for the next visit.

Numerous fathers did continue to endure the strains of at least occasional visits. Others, however, viewed the logistical and emotional tensions of visits to be sufficient or further cause for moving toward postdivorce absence. Several, for whom visits were consistently stressful and tense, had begun to deliberately avoid their offspring, screening telephone calls through answering machines and canceling or neglecting to arrange visits.

Interpersonal and emotional conflicts over children also involved the men's feelings of resentment at their perceived marginalization from family relationships. Given their respective primary family activities during marriage, in which they had been primary providers and their wives, even when employed, the primary parent and family caretaker, their parental relationships with their children differed from those of their former wives.[5] Mothers' relationships with children were relatively independent, whereas fathers' relationships with children involved the mother who typically played a mediating role. Consequently, mother-child relations often were viewed as being more durable and able to withstand the transitions and tensions inherent in the divorcing processes. These perceptions were reinforced by the men's place in a gender-structured society, their general acceptance of conventional gender beliefs and stereotypes, knowledge of the widespread prevalence of maternal custody after divorce, and personal experiences with postdivorce relations. After divorce, noncustodial fathers' parental authority and responsibilities in the routines of everyday life decreased, whereas the custodial mothers' increased. Former wives were deeply resented, especially

by noncustodial fathers who perceived them to have gained dispro-
portionate and undue amounts of power in the postdivorce family
situation.

Absence was a strategy of emotion management for some fathers
in response to feeling unappreciated or outrightly rejected by their
children, particularly older children who were more likely to enter
into the ongoing parental conflicts. Some children "took sides," seeking to explain or defend their mothers' actions. Others expressed
anger or resentment about the economic conditions facing them in
the postdivorce situation, implying that their fathers were responsible, sometimes for capricious or vengeful reasons, for the reduced
standard of living experienced after divorce. Most commonly, fathers
perceived that children were resentful through unspoken messages
conveyed, particularly through actions indicating sullen attitudes. On
the other hand, a few children behaved "too well," as if they were
"guests" during visits; such behaviors were interpreted by fathers to
mean that the parent-child relationship was being denied, even if
subtly, by the children. Because these fathers typically were unwilling
or uncertain about how to engage their children in verbal self-disclo-
sure about their feelings, the tensions between them and the fathers'
feelings of rejection increased over time rather than lessened. Absence
became a viable response.

Children were active agents in the postdivorce situation in other
ways as well. For example, several men's children under the age of 5
actively resisted leaving their homes or their mothers to go for visits,
crying and physically fighting when forcibly taken. Although one of
these fathers was engaged in a custody challenge, the other two were
considering full withdrawal from their children's lives, believing that
even at their young ages these children were deliberately rejecting
them as fathers. Four older children, ranging from ages 10 to 18,
refused to have any contact with their fathers, although, in each of
these cases, their siblings remained involved. Merged with these
fathers' feelings of anger about the rejection by one of their children
was fear that their other children would also come to refuse further

contact, influenced by the other sibling. Yet no concrete actions had been taken by these fathers to alter the situation.

Nearly all fathers who were dissatisfied with their visitation experiences, a large majority of those in the study, targeted the former wife as being responsible for the strained father-child relationships, believing that the stress and awkwardness of the visits could be eased by her intervention with the children.[6] The expectation that she facilitate the postdivorce relationship was an extension of the marital division of labor in which women are the emotional caretakers or workers (Hochschild, 1983; Riessman, 1990). That the former wife refused to continue serving as family mediator as she had during marriage was interpreted by these fathers as evidence of her misuse of power, intended deliberately to undermine or push him outside the bounds of postdivorce family relationships. For fathers who desired a meaningful relationship with their children in the postdivorce situation, the consequences of not having been a primary caretaker or full coparent during the marriage and being relatively inexperienced in handling the emotional dimensions of family life were pronouncedly adverse.

Prior family relationships, however powerful they were in shaping most of postdivorce ones, did not inevitably dictate them. While gender is relevant in men's parenting activities in that it places them into one of two possible structural locations, a change in status and thus change in experiences and expectations can lead to a change in parenting behaviors (Cohen, 1989; Risman, 1989). Ten of the men participating in the study, all but two of whom can be characterized as "androgynous" postdivorce fathers, marveled at how they had "learned to become a father only after divorcing." Each of the ten men had experienced emotional turmoil and confusion in the early days of being a divorced father, like the others. But they, as one noncustodial father of two children described the process, "had refused to drown and instead learned to swim, and even swim well." Meeting the challenges of being a divorced father was rewarding and satisfying; absence was personally inconceivable. Six of these ten fathers noted that the divorce experience had necessitated significant changes in their own behaviors without which they would not have become involved fathers. One said,

> If I hadn't divorced, I probably would have gone on in the same old way, relating to my kids as my father related to me and my sisters. He was just sort of there, in our lives, but not relating to us in any important ways. I would probably never have learned how to be a father.

Most fathers, however, were emotionally disconcerted about the quality of their relations with, or absence from, their children. They felt emotionally isolated, unable or unwilling to express their feelings about their children with others. Men who had remarried felt less emotionally isolated overall but half of those eighteen felt constrained in revealing the scope of their feelings about their children from the prior marriage to their present wives. The men's sense of isolation, together with the gamut of emotions experienced, led many to believe that men are the unrecognized emotional victims of divorce. One father, who had likened the success of his child snatching to the dropping of an A-bomb, bluntly summed up his observation that men are victimized by divorce:

> I learned we men have to be willing to eat the hurt. I'm very strong. But they beat us down so far. And they just keep beating. So the average guy just severs ties and leaves. He stops payments too. Even the payments are too painful a connection. It's just easier to eat the hurt and walk away. These fellahs go, just to survive. That's what I did. I had to survive. I left.

While on the one hand expressing pride in his aggressiveness and interactional tactics and on the other claiming to have been victimized, this father, like most, did not make any significant link between his actions and the persistently high levels of conflict and tension in the postdivorce situation. Nor did he see a relationship between his behaviors and his former wife's enormous distrust of his motives. Absent in a large majority of men's accounts was recognition that the character of the postdivorce situation, which extracted such a high emotional toll, was the outcome of collective activity in which they were primary participants.

Absence as a Standard of Comparison

The second facet of the phenomenon of postdivorce fatherhood was absence as a standard of comparison: absent fathers were the primary comparison group of divorced men for 80 percent of the fathers in this study. That so many fathers perceived absence to be a viable option for themselves partially explains the use of absent fathers as a reference. Also, most knew few if any divorced fathers who were extensively involved with their children; even custodial fathers knew almost no other men whose situations were similar to their own. All the interviewees, however, personally knew men who were totally absent from their children's lives, and their actions and situations were used for comparisons. Any involvement with their own children was evidence of good effort compared to absent fathers as was suggested in the descriptive terms frequently used to refer to absent fathers: *derelict dads, deadbeat dad,* and *bums*. Involvement of any kind rather than absence prompted a stance of self-congratulation among some fathers. For instance,

> I occasionally have to acknowledge that maybe I could have handled most of this better—better for my children—by not insisting on having the last word always with my ex. But at least I haven't checked out like lots of guys in my situation here. I've hung in there and struggled. But most guys just leave, hang it up and leave.

Several men who both used father absence as a reference and expressed an understanding of it, nonetheless condemned the practice. Those who expressed the harshest condemnation of absent fathers, however, were the men who had most successfully dictated the terms of their divorce settlement and child custody arrangements. Able to assert themselves because of their particular access to power and resources, they were critical of other divorced fathers who, they argued, needed to exert more effort and assertiveness to shape the postdivorce situation: they needed simply to be more "manly."

One father whose remarks about absent fathers were consistently derogatory was particularly satisfied with his postdivorce situation; he credited the outcome of his divorce to both his personal competence and assertiveness in dealing with his attorneys and to the coercive and intimidating approach he had used in interacting with his former wife. By threatening her with a legal battle for sole custody and drawing on his extensive business-related legal network, he had obtained shared physical as well as shared legal custody of their four-year-old daughter, an atypical custody arrangement in New York State, especially given the child's age. He had also successfully arranged the property settlement so as "to avoid ever having to pay child support," even though his former wife's income and earning potential were far less than his.

> I refused to let anyone but me set the terms of this divorce. I refused to be a part-time father. And I swore that I absolutely never, never would pay a cent in child support. So I found the hottest lawyer in the state and that's what we got.

The majority of fathers in the study, however, did not have the means to impose their desired divorce outcomes unilaterally and, for the most part, they sympathized, and often identified, with the experiences and choices of fathers who become absent. The absent fathers constituted a primary comparison group for these divorced men suggests basic questions about the meaning of fathering to them in general. Fatherhood as a status within an intact marriage and family had a relatively clear definition, but fathering as an array of activities, interactional processes, and particular kinds of social relations between father and child was ambiguous, at best, to many.

☺ Conclusion

Family transitions prompted gender role and identity transitions in these men's lives. Indeed, much of the apparently intransigent hold of the masculinist discourse of divorce on the majority of men interviewed (many of whom seemed to respond to the stresses and turmoil of divorce by resorting to more traditional or conventional masculine behaviors and perspectives than they had while married) was aimed at reestablishing or buttressing the masculine self as a dominant self amidst the array of changes prompted by divorce. A primary theme of the discourse was a rhetoric of rights through which relationships, actions, and emotions were framed and defined. Absence was understood as a viable response to certain interactional and emotional situations. The possibility that father absence was dysfunctional in that it foreclosed opportunities for negotiating more meaningful relations with children was largely unacknowledged by these fathers, especially since involvement took a variety of forms, many of which were not fully distinct from absence. Rather than being "locked out" of postdivorce relationships with their children by others, as has been suggested by various speculative explanations for father absence (Bauer & Bauer, 1985; Doyle, 1985), these fathers were more typically "locked in" to particular relational configurations and systems of meanings held by them and shaped by gendered ideology, practices, and social arrangements. These perspectives often countered the development of continuing and reciprocally nurturant postdivorce relationships with their children and contributed, instead, to the acceptance of father absence as an understandable, if sometimes regrettable, practice.

Endnotes

[1]Other but less common interpersonal conflicts to be avoided by father absence were ones involving a new spouse or companion, and, sometimes, additional children, hers and/or theirs. Logistical issues involving time, money, and geographical distance were also issues contributing to conflict and were to be avoided. Since these issues were typically sub-

sumed under others, especially emotional or interpersonal conflicts with the former wife, they are not more fully developed in this article.

[2]According to the men in this study, numerous allegations had been made against them that behaviors toward a child during visits had constituted or approximated sexual molestation. Following formal investigations and hearings, one of these fathers was denied access to his children until they reached age 18 and could choose for themselves whether they wanted contact with their father. Another father gave as his explanation for his absence his fear that if he were again investigated he would be wrongfully convicted of child sexual molestation. Also, two fathers claimed that their children had been sexually molested by friends of the former wife and another by the maternal grandfather. One mother agreed voluntarily to prevent contact between the child and the suspect, and the other mother had denied and been cleared of all charges by an investigation through the New York Family Court. Nearly a fifth of all the men interviewed indicated they suspected that boyfriends of their former wife or her new husband engaged in activities of a sexual character with their children. These findings suggest, at the least, that the exchange of such allegations between divorced parents is widespread and that systematic research exploring this issue is needed.

[3]Visitation is recognized within the law as the means through which a divorced noncustodial parent retains access to minor children and visitation rights are closely protected by the judicial system in each state (Novinson, 1983). A schedule of visitation is typically stipulated in the divorce settlement approved or ordered by the court. Denial or interference with a noncustodial parent's access to minor children by the custodial parent is a violation of law: a noncustodial parent has specified and protected rights to his or her children. Judicial procedures for seeking enforcement of visitation rights and redress for violations are available in all states, and one possible sanction for interfering with visitation is the loss of custody. In contrast to these specified parental rights, there are no legal mandates requiring a parent to become or remain involved with a child (Bruch, 1983; Polikoff, 1983).

[4]A direct relationship exists between the nonpayment of child support and paternal absence: fathers paying no support having particularly low levels of contact with their children. It is the fact of support, not the amount, which is related to maintaining ties with children (Furstenberg et al.,

1983, 663; see also Hoffman & Duncan, 1988; Weitzman, 1985). Payment of child support is not related to socioeconomic or income status (Chambers, 1979; Weitzman, 1985). Moreover, men's economic situations are not altered markedly by the payment of child support. In sharp contrast to women's—and therefore most children's—postdivorce circumstances, men's standard of living actually improves after divorce (Corcoran, Duncan, & Hill, 1984; Hoffman & Duncan, 1988; Weitzman, 1985).

[5]Despite some changes in the "good provider role" (Bernard, 1981), the increased family involvement of some fathers (Pleck, 1985, 1989), and much rhetoric about the "new father," the vast majority of men (in intact families) retain primary responsibility for economic support and have relatively limited involvement with their children (Lamb, 1986; Lamb, Pleck, & Levine, 1986).

[6]Only a small proportion of divorced spouses develop a cooperative, even friendly, relationship with each other, indicating that the "pattern of cooperative parenting, so widely portrayed in the popular media, is, in fact, rather rare" (Furstenberg & Nord, 1985, 899). Indeed, former spouses appear to be "reluctant partners in the childrearing process," and children often provide the link between the parents in terms of communication (Furstenberg & Nord, 1985, 900).

References

Arendell, T. Forthcoming. *Fathers and divorce* (tentative title). Berkeley: University of California Press.

Bauer, B., & Bauer, D. (1985). Visitation lawsuit. In F. Baumi (Ed.), *Men freeing men.* Jersey City, NJ: New Atlantis.

Bernard. J. (1985). The good-provider rule: Its rise and fall. *American Psychologist, 36,* 1–12.

Bordieu, P. (1987). *Outline of a theory of practice.* Cambridge: Cambridge University Press.

Bruch, C. (1983). Developing normative standards for child-support payments: A critique of current practice. In J. Cassetty (Ed.), *The parental child-support obligation.* Lexington, MA: Lexington Books.

Chambers, D. (1979). *Making fathers pay: The enforcement of child support.* Chicago: University of Chicago Press.

Cohen, T. (1989). Becoming and being husbands and fathers: Work and family conflict for men. In B. Risman & P. Schwartz (Eds.), *Gender in intimate relationships*. Belmont, CA: Wadsworth.

Corcoran, M., Duncan, G., & Hill, M. (1984). The economic fortunes of women and children: Lessons from the panel study of income dynamics. *Signs: Journal of Women in Culture and Society, 10*(2): 232–248.

Doyle, R. (1985). Divorce. In F. Baumli (Ed.), *Men freeing men*. Jersey City, NJ: New Atlantis.

Emery, R. (1988). *Marriage, divorce, and children's adjustment*. Newbury Park, CA: Sage.

Furstenberg, F., & Nord, C. (1985). Parenting apart: Patterns of childrearing after marital disruption. *Journal of Marriage and Family, 47*, 893–904.

Furstenberg, F., Nord, C., Peterson, J., & Zill, N. (1983). The life course of children of divorce: Marital disruption and parental contact. *American Sociological Review, 8*, 656–668.

Hochschild, A. (1983). *The managed heart: Commercialization of human feeling*. Berkeley: University of California Press.

Hochschild, A. (1990). *Ideology and emotion management: A perspective and path for future research*. Department of Sociology, University of California, Berkeley.

Hoffman, S., & Duncan, G. (1988). What are the economic consequences of divorce? *Demography, 25*, 415–427.

Jaggar, A. (1983). *Feminist politics and human nature*. Totowa, NJ: Rowman & Allenheld.

Lamb, M. (1986). *The father's role: Applied perspectives*. New York: Wiley.

Lamb, M., Pleck, J., & Levine, J. (1986). Effects of increased paternal involvement on children in two-parent families. In R. Lewis & R. Salt (Eds.), *Men in families*. Beverly Hills, CA: Sage.

Novinson, S. (1983). Post-divorce visitation: Untying the triangular knot. *University of Illinois Law Review, 1*, 121–200.

Pleck, J. (1985). *Working wives, working husbands*. Beverly Hills, CA: Sage.

Pleck, J. (1989). Men's power with women, other men, and society: A men's movement and analysis. In M. Kimmel & M. Messner (Eds.), *Men's lives*. New York: Macmillan.

Polikoff, N. (1983). Gender and child-custody determinations: Exploding the myths. In I. Diamond (Ed.), *Families, politics, and public policy*. New York: Longman.

Riessman, C. K. (1990). *Divorce talks: Women and men make sense of personal relationships*. New Brunswick, NJ: Rutgers University Press.

Risman, B. (1989). Can men "mother"? Life as a single father. In B. Risman & P. Schwartz (Eds.), *Gender in intimate relationships*. Belmont, CA: Wadsworth.

Swidler, A. (1986). Culture in action—symbols and strategies. *American Sociological Review, 51*, 273–286.

Weitzman, L. (1985). *The divorce revolution: The unexpected social and economic consequences for women and children in America*. New York: Free Press.

⊚   ⊚   ⊚

Questions

1. How did the men in this study explain their post-divorce absent-father status?

2. What are fathers' rights? What activities did the men in this study engage in to secure these rights?

3. Why was child support such a matter of contention for divorced fathers? Do you think that child support would be an equally contentious matter for divorced mothers? Explain why or why not.

4. How did divorce affect some men's sense of masculinity? What did these men do to reestablish their sense of masculinity?

5. How might the legal system make divorce less stressful for ex-spouses? What should the courts do to keep embattled former spouses from using their children as pawns?

Dilemmas of Involved Fatherhood

KATHLEEN GERSON

Why are some men actively involved as fathers, while many others are not? What social arrangements make it difficult for men to be involved with their children? In the article below, Kathleen Gerson uses qualitative data from her research on primarily white, middle-class, and working-class men to explain the dilemmas faced by involved fathers. She also shows how current economic, social, and ideological arrangements make it difficult for men to be actively engaged in raising their children.

Work's a necessity, but the things that really matter are spending time with my family. If I didn't have a family, I don't know what I would have turned to. That's why I say you're rich in a lot of ways other than money. I look at my daughter and think, "My family is everything."

Carl, a thirty-four-year-old utilities worker

· · ·

Social disapproval and economic inequality put full-time domesticity out of reach for almost all men. Yet most also found that economic necessity and employer intransigence made anything less than full-time work an equally distant possibility. Few employers offered the option of part-time work, especially in male-dominated fields. Arthur, a married sanitation worker planning for fatherhood, complained:

> If it was feasible, I would love to spend more time with my child. That would be more important to me than working. I'd love to be able to work twenty-five hours a week or four days a week and have three days off to spend with the family, but most jobs aren't going to accommodate you that way.

Yet, even if part-time work were available, involved fathers still needed the earnings that only full-time and overtime work could offer. Lou, the sewage worker who worked the night shift in order to spend days with this young daughter, could not accept lower wages or fewer benefits:

> If I knew that financially everything would be set, I'd stay home. I'd like to stay more with my daughter. It's a lot of fun to be with a very nice three-year-old girl, but if I work less, I would equate it to less money and then I wouldn't be taking care of my family. If it meant less work and the same or more money, I'd say, "Sure!" I'd be dumb if I didn't.

Dean, the driver for a city department of parks, agreed that his economic obligations could not take a backseat to his nurturing ones:

> It always comes down to the same thing: I would like to have more time to spend with my children, but if I didn't have money, what's the sense of having time off? If I could work part-time and make enough money, that would be fine and dandy.

Since involved fathers tried to nurture as well as support their children, they made an especially hard choice between money and time. Like many mothers, they had to add caretaking onto full-time workplace responsibilities, but employers are generally reluctant to recognize male (or female) parental responsibility as a legitimate right or need. Worse yet, paternal leaves are rarely considered a legitimate option for men even if they formally exist. Involved fathers wished to take time off for parenting, but like most men they were reluctant to do so for fear of imperiling their careers.[1] And even though most employers allow health-related leaves with impunity, they have not been so flexible when it comes to the job of parenting. Workers receive the message that illness is unavoidable, but parenting is voluntary—an indication of a lack of job commitment. Our current corporate culture thus makes parenting hazardous to anyone's career, and choosing a "daddy track" can be just as dangerous as the much-publicized "mommy track." Juan, a financial analyst, knew he could not pull back from his job for more than a few days or a week without jeopardizing his job security. To parental leave:

> I'd say yes, but realistically no. It would be a problem because it's very difficult for me to tell my boss that I have to leave at such a time. I have deadlines to meet. If I leave the office for two or three months, my job is in jeopardy.

Because employers did not offer flexible options for structuring work on a daily basis or over the course of a career, some involved fathers looked to self-employment or home-based work for more flexibility and control. Craig, the ex-dancer currently working in an office, hoped he would be able to integrate work and parenting by working at home:

> I would like to find myself in the situation where I'm not locked into a nine-to-five schedule. Ultimately, I hope I'm doing consulting on my own at home, which means time close to the family. So that in the middle of my own workday, at the house, I'm available. I can just put my work aside and play Daddy.

Most could not even entertain this option. They had to fit parenting in around the edges of their work lives.

Domestic arrangements also impeded full equality. Child rearing remains an undervalued, isolating, and largely invisible accomplishment for *all* parents. This has fueled women's flight from domesticity and also dampened men's motivation to choose it. Russell, the legal-aid attorney and father of two, recognized that child rearing was less valued than employment:

I think I would feel somewhat meaningless to not be engaged in any form of productive work—although certainly raising children is productive work. But I couldn't be responsible for that on a full-time basis. While I love my guys, I don't think I could be around them all the time.

Child rearing can be invisible as well as undervalued. Unlike the size of a paycheck or the title one holds at work, there are few socially recognized rewards for the time a parent devotes to raising a child or the results it produces. This made only the most dedicated, like Hank, willing to consider full-time parenting:

Nobody will know the time and the effort I put in the family. They will look down on it. I would devote time, hours, and nobody will be happy with it except me because I'll know what I was trying for.

The forces pulling women out of the home are stronger than the forces pulling men into it. Since the social value of public pursuits outstrips the power and prestige of private ones, men are likely to resist full-time domesticity even as women move toward full-time employment. This process is similar to the one pulling women into male-dominated occupations while leaving men less inclined to enter female-dominated ones. In addition, just as women in male-dominated occupations face prejudice and discrimination, fathers who become equal or primary parents are stigmatized—treated as "tokens" in a female-dominated world. Roger shied away from the pervasive questioning about his life as a custodial parent:

I think I've become somewhat more introverted than I used to be—because I get tired of explaining my situation at home. . . . The thing that blows all the kids' minds—they're all living with Mommy and my kids are living with Daddy.

In the face of such disincentives, most involved fathers rejected staying home for the same reasons many women do and more. Female breadwinning and male homemaking did not seem acceptable even when they made economic sense. Robin, a stockbroker, rejected domesticity precisely because his poor work prospects left him in no state to bear the additional stigma of becoming a house-husband. Although he was making a lot less money than his wife was, he felt too "demoralized" to consider staying home. "I'm not secure enough, I guess, to stay home and be a househusband."

Of course, involved fathers actively resisted the discrimination they encountered. They asserted their nurturing competence and insisted on being taken as seriously as female parents are. The pre-vailing skepticism about men's parental abilities, however, made this an uphill battle. Ernie complained:

> I believe I have as much right in raising the child as she does, but I found a lot of reverse discrimination—people assuming that the mother takes care of the child. It's a lot of stereotyp-ing, a lot that's taken for granted. Like pediatricians: they speak to my wife; they won't speak to me. I say, "Hey, I take care of her, too." They look at me like I'm invisible. The same thing with the nursery school. I went out on all the inter-views. They looked at me like, "What're *you* doing here?"

Economic, social, and ideological arrangements thus made involved fatherhood difficult. The lack of workplace and domestic supports diluted and suppressed the potential for involvement even among the most motivated men. In the absence of these hurdles, fathers who wished to be involved might have participated far more than they actually did. They might, in fact, have made choices that now remain open to a rapidly diminishing number of women. Ernie wished he had options that only full-time mothers enjoy:

> I'm not the type that has career aspirations and is very goal-oriented. If I didn't have to work, I wouldn't. But I would vol-unteer. I would work in a nursery school. I would do a lot more volunteer work with my daughter's school. I would love to go on trips like the mothers who don't work, be more active in the P.T.A. I would *love* that. But I can't.

As the supports for homemaking mothers erode, supports for equal and primary fathers have not emerged to offset the growing imbalance between children's needs and families' resources. Fathers have had to depend on paid help, relatives, and already overburdened wives even when they did not wish to do so.

These obstacles not only left mothers giving up more. They also made involved fathers appear heroic about *whatever* they did. Comparisons with other men could be used to ward off complaints and resist further change. Ernie maintained:

> Sometimes she didn't think I did enough. I couldn't stand that because I thought I was doing too much. I really felt I was doing more than I should, whatever that means. I told her to go talk to some of her friends and see what their husbands are doing.

Nurturing fathers faced deeply rooted barriers to full equality in parenting. Social arrangements at work and in the home dampened even willing men's ability to share equally. The truncated range of choices open to most of these men limited the options of their wives, ex-wives, and partners as well. We can only guess how many mothers' helpers would become equal parents if these obstacles did not exist or, better yet, were replaced by positive supports for involved fatherhood.

☻ Benefiting from the Loss of Privilege: Incentives for Change

If full equality remained beyond the reach of most involved fathers, they nevertheless moved a notable distance toward it. They were not simply forced to make concessions; nor were they just being altruistic. They also perceived offsetting, if unheralded, benefits. After all, parenting can be its own reward—offering intrinsic pleasures and a powerful sense of accomplishment. Rick explained:

> I have an extremely close relationship with my kids, and that makes me feel good. The fact that they're both doing very

well in school—I know that at least a little bit of that comes from having been with them when they were young. So there's all those interactions in seeing them on their way to being healthy and vibrant kids.

These feelings took on added significance when other avenues for building self-esteem were blocked. Todd, the aspiring actor who became a construction worker, hoped his talents could be channeled toward his daughter instead of his job:

If there's any Creator at all up there, She or It or They're going to ask for some sort of accounting at the end. They're going to be pleased if they gave you a certain amount of gifts and you were able to do something with them. I'd still like to be a part of something more meaningful than putting in a new fire hydrant—I guess through my influence on this little one's life.

If children offered a source of pride for those whose workplace aspirations had not been met, this was not just a concern for passing on genes or the family name. Contributions of time and emotions counted more. Carl, who chose utility repair work so that he could care for his daughter after school, saw his "investment" reflected in her talents and achievements:

I've had a lot of compliments on her, and I take them as a compliment also. It's something that became part of you— teaching them different things, helping them grow up. They'll do something, and it's like seeing a reflection of you.

As work opportunities stall in an age of stagnant economic growth, parenting offers men another avenue for developing self-esteem. But economically successful fathers also reaped benefits from involvement because it balanced lives that would otherwise have been more narrowly focused on paid work. For Charles, the attorney with a young son, caretaking provided a legitimate reason for limiting the demands of work: "I'm working a little less hard, taking on fewer responsibilities. . . . But I think it's great. I don't need all the other shit."

Children also provided the hope of permanence in an age of divorce: Even happily married fathers came to see their children as the bedrock of stability in a shaky world, the one bond that could not be severed or assailed. Having been reared by a single mother, Juan viewed his children rather than his wife as the best chance for enduring emotional ties: "What if one day my wife and I get sick of each other after so many years? So I would like to have children."

Involved fatherhood also provided emotional supports by creating a bond between husbands and wives. Married men were less likely to feel rejected by their wives and excluded from the new relationships that form with the birth of a child. Timothy, the worker at a city dump, could not understand why less involved fathers complained of being rejected when a new baby arrived:

> They have these books about how fathers are supposed to go through blues because the wife is giving her attention to the child. Is this some kind of maniac that wrote this? I take care of him just as much as she does.

Sharing the load of caring for a newborn also seemed to decrease the chances that a mother would feel overwhelmed and alone during a critical, and trying, turning point in a marriage. Carlos hoped that sharing the caretaking would help him avoid the hostility that he felt unequal arrangements would generate:

> I think it's a great burden to have one parent do all the caretaking. It would burn out that person, and they're not going to be able to respond to you. Then I would start feeling resentment towards her and possible the child. So the only way I could see avoiding that is by sharing the responsibility.

Since involved fathers believed that a satisfying relationship depended on both partners being able to meet their needs, thwarting a partner's dreams by refusing to participate seemed to be a Pyrrhic victory. The costs of *not* sharing appeared greater than the costs of sharing. Carl was pleased to escape his parents' pattern:

My parents are the old school. He never really touched a dish. I like what I'm doing better. The older way, I feel the woman will think, "I never really had an opportunity to do things." She will become resentful later on. Where my wife can't say nothing because she's had her freedom, she's worked, she's not stayed in the kitchen barefoot and pregnant, and I did what I had to do. I feel in the long run it pays off. The other way, maybe she would have left.

Involved fatherhood thus offered two ways of coping with the risks of marriage in an era of divorce. It provided another source of emotional sustenance in the event that the marital bond did not survive. And it offered a way to build less rancorous relationships by reducing wives' resentment. Indeed, there is growing evidence that egalitarian relationships do provide benefits to husbands and wives. In one report, wives whose husbands participated in domestic duties showed lower rates of depression than those with husbands who don't, while another found that the more housework a husband does, the lower are the chances that his wife has considered divorce.[2]

Emotional gratification and marital peace were not the only payoffs. In agreeing to share the domestic load, men can also share the economic load. Their wives' income lessens the pressure to work long hours and take on second jobs. Wesley was pleased to exchange extra hours at work for domestic sharing:

If Cindy wants to be home, she can stay home. But that would probably mean I would have to either get myself another job or work overtime on the job I have. I would do it. She knows that. But she doesn't want me to. We spend more time with each other this way.

Involved fathers also believed their children would benefit in both the short and long runs—perceptions that research on both married and divorced fathers supports. Larry observed:

Having spent a lot of time with both of us, she's not really dependent on either one of us. Mommy's like daddy; daddy's like mommy. At times I *am* her mother. It's good to switch roles. She don't run to mommy or run to daddy. She runs to both of us.

They hoped their example would help their daughters and sons develop a flexible approach to building their own lives. Ernie decided his involvement created a better domestic environment for his daughter:

The sharing—it's a good role model for her. She sees me cook. I'm trying to teach her baking, and I think it's nice my daughter is learning baking from her father. So I'm hoping she sees that it's split and not that just the wife does this and the man does that.

He also hoped his participation would give his daughter a sense of self-reliance, agreeing with a growing group of psychologists who argue that girls no less than boys need their fathers. Both sexes identify in varying degrees with both parents, and girls look to fathers as well as mothers to provide models for living:[3]

Raising my child, that is my priority—seeing that she's raised well in the sense of preparing her to face the world, trying to get her exposed as much as possible, so she may find out what she likes to pursue. I hope she has a career. I hope she finds something she really likes and works for it.

These men concluded that their domestic arrangements would also benefit their sons, echoing recent research showing that sons of involved fathers are likely to show a more developed capacity for empathy.[4] Wesley thus concluded that his two sons "feel close to the two of us. Maybe when they get married, they'll share in the house."

Just as these fathers created families that differed from the households in which they were reared, so their children will take the lessons of their childhood into unknown futures. Involved fathers' belief in the advantages of domestic sharing cannot guarantee a similar response in their children, but it can and did strengthen their own resolve to create a more egalitarian household. As more fathers became involved, their growing numbers should prompt wider social acceptance of egalitarian households, bolstering the option to make such choices.

Ultimately, however, men's movement toward domestic equality will depend on their ability to overcome the obstacles to change and their desire to resist the social pressures to conform. Equal fathers were willing and able to defy social expectations, to overcome social constraints, and to reject the pathways of the past. There is good reason to believe that their outlooks and choices reflect a simmering mood among many American men, who long for more work flexibility and fewer work demands. There is even reason to believe many would be willing to relinquish some earnings in exchange for spending more time with their families. A *Time* survey found that 56% of a random sample of men said they would forfeit up to one-fourth of their salaries "to have more family and personal time," and 45% "said they would probably refuse a promotion that involved sacrificing hours with their families."[5] Carl reflects this mood:

> It's amazing how many people don't understand the way I feel. I would prefer to be home than work overtime, where they would kill to get it. They say, "What are you, rich?" No, but you only need a certain amount of money to live. God forbid you walk down the street and get struck by a car, or whatever, and it's over. I don't want to say, "Why didn't I spend more time with my family?" It's not going to happen to me. You can control it.

By focusing on the advantages and discounting the drawbacks of their choices, men are able to overcome some of the social and ideological barriers to equal parenting. In adding up the sacrifices and the gains, Larry spoke for the group: "I've given some things up, sure, but the changes in my lifestyle are eighty or ninety percent in the positive."

Though few in number, equal fathers demonstrate that men can discover or acquire nurturing skills and find pleasure in using them. Those men who did find support for being an equal father made contingent choices just like those who did not. In both instances, different circumstances could easily have produced different outcomes. It is not surprising that Rick found his rare and unexpected path to be a matter of chance:

> I have very conservative attitudes in many respects. The fact that we got married and had children was very conservative. The fact that within those parameters, we shared, co-shared, work and family—that was not conservative. We've never discussed it, but I feel that the outcome is built much more on chance. I may not have always felt that way, but my own experiences confirmed it.

Chance, however, is just another way of saying that his choice was based on unusual and unexpected opportunities. Given how rare are the supports for involved fathering and how pervasive the obstacles, its rise is even more significant than its limited nature. For the potential of the many men who wish to be more involved to be realized, however, the unusual circumstances that now prompt only a small fraction of men to become equal parents must become real for a much larger group.

Endnotes

[1]Pleck, 1993.

[2]Huber & Spitze, 1983; Ross, Mirowsky, & Huber, 1983.

[3]Secunda, 1992.

[4]Goleman, 1990.

[5]Reported in Stacey, 1991.

References

Goleman, D. (1990a, January 16). Men at 65: Surprising findings about emotional well-being. *New York Times*, C1, 12.

Goleman, D. (1990b, July 10). Surprising findings about the development of empathy in children. *New York Times*, C1.

Huber, J., & Spitze, G. (1983). *Sex stratification: Children, housework, and jobs*. New York: Academic Press.

Pleck, J. H. (1983). Husbands' paid work and family roles: Current research trends. *Research in the Interweave of Social Roles: Jobs and Families, 3,* 251–333.

Secunda, V. (1992). *Women and their fathers: The sexual and romantic impact of the first man in your life.* New York: Delacorte Press.

Stacey, J. (1991). Backwards toward the post-modern family. In A. Wolfe (Ed.), *America at century's end* (pp. 17–34). Berkeley and Los Angeles: University of California Press.

◉ ◉ ◉

Questions

1. What are some factors that make it difficult for men to be actively involved with their children?

2. Gerson argues that "the forces pulling women out of the home are stronger than the forces pulling men into it." Explain what she means by this statement.

3. Describe three of the benefits of being an involved father.

4. Describe your father's level of involvement in your life when you were young. Use what you learned in this article to help account for his level of participation in your upbringing.

The Portrayal of Men's Family Roles in Television Commercials

GAYLE KAUFMAN
Davidson College

Studies show that the average American watches thirty hours of television each week—including over 500 commercials—and that portrayals of men and women in commercials are heavily gender stereotyped. Social scientists studying commercial content and images have concentrated primarily on how gender is portrayed at various times of day, associated with various product types, in various locations, and engaged in various domestic activities. In this article, Gayle Kaufman expands on this research by focusing on how men and women are shown interacting with children in television commercials.

There have been a number of changes in the structure of the family, including increases in age at marriage, decreases in number of children, and increases in divorce (Cherlin, 1992). Along with these changes, there has been a tremendous increase in female employment, especially among mothers (U.S. Bureau of the Census, 1995). By the mid 1980s, only 10% of families were traditional families in which the father worked while the mother stayed home to take care of the children (Levitan, Belous, and Gallo, 1988). Women have been expanding their roles to include working outside the home as well as being wives and mothers. At the same time, men's involvement in more domestic roles has increased (Gershuny and Robinson, 1988), but at a slower pace than women's entrance into the labor market. Goldscheider and Waite (1991) find that wives do four-fifths of the cooking, laundry, and shopping as well as two-thirds of the child care, cleaning, and dishwashing. Household maintenance and yard work are the only tasks that are not done mainly by wives. Even when wives work outside the home, they perform more housework than husbands (Demo and Acock, 1993).

Still, studies suggest that the image of an involved family man has become increasingly popular. Pleck (1987) describes these new fathers as being more involved than previously, participating in child care as well as play activities. However, several researchers have noted the speedier changes in image than in actual behavior (LaRossa, 1988; Thompson and Walker, 1989) and the overstated changes described in popular accounts (Demo and Acock, 1993). Others have suggested that the new father image is an ideological construct based on middle- or upper-middle-class men (Messner, 1993). This study seeks to explore further men's family image, and whether that image is of an involved family man, by examining the portrayal of men in family roles, as fathers and husbands, on television commercials.

Viewing men's family roles in commercials is important because Americans are extensively exposed to the influential images of commercials. In 1 week, Americans watch an average of more than 30 hours of television (Kellner, 1990; Signorelli, 1991) and see over 500 commercials (Bretl and Cantor, 1988). With this constant barage of images, it is no surprise that researchers have found a connection between commercials and gender role attitudes. Commercials can influence the gender socialization process (Blakeney, Barnes, and McKeough, 1983). The portrayal of women in stereotypically traditional roles may encourage or validate attitudes that are supportive of more traditional roles for women even if women's television roles do not correspond to their roles in real life (Signorielli, 1990), and the effect on female adolescents' perceptions can be especially great (Perimenis, 1991; Tan, 1979). Television seems to play an important role in shaping children's attitudes. Commercials have a detrimental effect on elementary school children's views of women's occupational roles, and girls may even change their occupation preference to ones portrayed by women in commercials (O'Bryant and Corder-Bolz, 1978). In addition, exposure to television among children increases attitudes that stereotype gender roles (Kimball, 1986).

However, society also appears to influence the content of commercials, with gender role stereotypes being more prevalent in more patriarchal societies (Huang, 1995). Whether commercials influence society or society influences commercials, there is a connection between popular thinking and the media. This paper focuses on the presence of men in families on television commercials and how they are portrayed, whether they are involved or uninvolved, what kinds of activities they are involved in, and how these activities vary depending on the age and gender of the children with them. Often the goal of commercials is to get viewers to want to be like the people in the commercials and therefore to want the product. How men are portrayed in commercials may have a profound impact on the way people think about gender roles and their view of themselves and others. Indeed, a recent study by Garst and Bodenhausen (1997) finds that at least nontraditional men's attitudes are influenced by exposure to traditionally masculine models in magazine advertisements. As men's roles at home changes, men may look to others for role standards. One possible source for this is television.

❧ Men's Family Roles

Although fathers have been seen mainly as providers since the industrial revolution took them out of the home, their role is evolving again as greater expectations to be engaged with their children arise (Rossi, 1984). However, fathers still spend much less time than mothers caring for children (Berk, 1985). When wives work outside the home, both husbands and children increase their share of household tasks (Goldscheider and Waite, 1991), but much of the increase in fathers' proportion of child care is due to mothers decreasing their time rather than fathers increasing their absolute time (Parke and Stearns, 1993). LaRossa (1988) argues that although there have been changes in the culture of fatherhood, the behavior of fathers has not really changed.

Parke and Stearns (1993, p. 166) suggest that although modern fathers are more involved with their children, their role is still seen as one of supporter: "Fathers have moved into a more prominent supporting-actor stance, rather than earning equal billing with mothers." Fathers "help" with parenting but mothers are never seen in this way (Ross, Mirowsky, and Huber, 1983). Mothers have a responsibility for their children that is exclusive and constant (Boulton, 1983), and they spend much more time alone with their children than do fathers (Baruch and Barnett, 1983).

However, there is no indication that men cannot care for infants; rather, Lamb, Frodi, Hwang, and Frodi (1982) find that fathers are as competent as mothers. Men are helping more in the birthing of their children and increasingly are attending their wives' deliveries (Lewis, 1986). Men are also becoming more active in the child-rearing process. Fathers are now more likely to attend to their baby in the middle of the night and put their children to bed. However, there has not been much change in the amount of time spent bathing and changing diapers (Lewis, 1986).

Men are increasingly viewing children as companions, providing love and enjoyment as men teach them and experience their growth (Veroff, Douvan, and Kulka, 1981). Signs that support for fathering is increasing are that there is more support for fathers' involvement, increasing advice for fathers in the media, increasing prenatal classes where fathers are involved, and increasing support for involvement of fathers in the birth process (Parke and Stearns, 1993). In popular magazines, parenting is increasingly thought of as gender-free rather than just as mothering (Atkinson and Blackwelder, 1993).

❧ Past Literature on Men in Television

In the past, men have often been portrayed as incompetent husbands and fathers on television. In an article entitled "Better Dead than Wed," Pollner (1982) discusses the negative portrayal of married men as compared to single men on television. Married men were seen as vulnerable and trapped, relying on wives to tell them what to do. Single men were portrayed positively as being free, happy, and leading exciting lives. The implication for young boys was clear: be like the bachelors (Pollner, 1982).

Stereotypical portrayals of men's and women's roles still persist (Lovdal, 1989). Coltrane and Allan (1994) find little change between the 1950s and the 1980s in men's image. Although more recently men and women appear nearly equally often in prime time commercials (Bretl and Cantor, 1988), their roles still differ. Men are more likely to be employed while women are more likely to be spouses or parents, apparently with no other occupation (that is not to say that they have no occupation but that occupation does not come into play). However, there has been an increase in men shown as spouses and parents (Bretl and Cantor, 1988). Men are still more likely to be away from home and outdoors and to be advertising products used outside the home (Bretl and Cantor, 1988), and they are not often portrayed as nurturing parents (Coltrane and Allan, 1994). In contrast, women are more likely to be advertising products used at home (Bretl and Cantor, 1988).

More specifically, women are likely to appear in commercials for over the counter drugs. They are often portrayed as experts, as husbands and children look to wives and mothers for help. The message is that women are nurturers and are needed to take care of the family. On the other hand, men are either absent or portrayed as dependent on women and childlike, but at the same time, this portrayal is exaggerated so as not to threaten men. All of this reinforces the image of women staying home to take care of the family (Craig, 1992a). When prime-time commercials are compared to commercials aired during the afternoon or weekend, different images emerge. Daytime advertisements focus on products and settings associated with home, family, and housewives (e.g., cooking, cleaning, and child care). Men do not appear often but when they do they are portrayed in positions of authority. In contrast, weekend advertisements focus on life away from family and home, often excluding women and children and playing on male fantasy and escapism (Craig, 1992b). Men appear more and speak more in commercials aired during Sunday football games (Riffe, Place, and Mayo, 1993). Compared to daytime and weekend advertisements, women have more authority while men are more likely to be spouses or parents in prime time commercials (Craig, 1992b).

International studies also show differences in the roles men and women play on television. In British television commercials, men are more likely to do voice overs (speaking part with no appearance), be an interviewer or narrator, be shown with a female background, and make an end comment (Furnham and Bitar, 1993). Women are more likely to be dependent and in the home (Manstead and McCulloch, 1981). This gender role stereotyping is present in British radio advertisements as well as in television commercials (Furnham and Schofield, 1986). In Australian television advertisements, men and women are also often depicted in stereotypical roles. Women are more likely to be portrayed as "dependent" (meaning here being a parent, spouse, partner, homemaker, or sex object) and more likely to be in the home than men (Mazzella, Durkin, Cerini, and Buralli, 1992).

Past research tells us that men are rarely shown in domestic or paternal roles. However, this paper goes beyond previous studies by not only examining gender differences in day part, product type, location, and domestic activities, but also differentiating between men and women with children. Further, the investigation of child care and other activities with children is enhanced by delving into the more complex patterns that occur when the research questions guide this study. How are men and women involved with children? In what kinds of activities do they participate? Does this participation vary depending on child's age and gender? Given past research, the following hypotheses are proposed.

1. Women are expected to be more involved with children, especially in child care tasks, than men.
2. Men will be more likely to play with children than care for them.

3. Men are expected to be more involved with male children than female children.

❧ Data and Method

Commercials were videotaped over a period of 1 week from November 12 to November 20, 1995. Twelve hours of three day parts—Sunday football, daytime, and prime time—were recorded in order to obtain a sample of commercials viewed to various extents by men and women. Commercials during Sunday football were recorded from 1:00 to 7:00 PM (Eastern time) on two consecutive Sundays. Each day 3 hours of NBC and 3 hours of FOX (the two stations that carried Sunday football at that time) were recorded. The three major networks (ABC, CBS, NBC) were represented twice each for both daytime and prime time. Daytime commercials were drawn solely from soap opera programs and were recorded from 2:00 to 4:00 PM on ABC and CBS for 2 weekdays each and from 1:00 to 3:00 PM on NBC for 2 weekdays. Prime-time commercials were recorded from 9:00 to 11:00 PM on ABC, CBS, and NBC, 2 nights each.

Only national commercials were selected. No local commercials, public service messages, or commercials for other television shows, movies, or videotapes were used in this analysis. This procedure resulted in 1061 commercials—277 during football, 529 during daytime, and 255 during prime time. This sample comes disproportionately from daytime commercials. This is probably due to the greater number of commercials shown during daytime than other times, given the same amount of time. All network commercials, including repeats, were coded. Exposure to an idea is the focus here and as such repeats were included (see Craig, 1992b). There were two coders for all commercials. To assess reliability, an agreement coefficient was calculated for each coding category (Krippendorff, 1980). The agreement coefficients were all greater than .98, indicating a high degree of reliability.

Central Figure

The unit of analysis is the individual character. Central figures are adults featured in a commercial. Up to two central figures were coded for each commercial. If there were more than two adults, the two most prominent were chosen for coding. Commercials in which there were no adult central figures were not coded. The resulting sample size of characters is 944. Most of these characters appear to come from a middle-class background and are non-Hispanic white, with an underrepresentation of minorities.

Family

Central figures were coded as either having a spouse/partner present or not. Central figures were also coded as having a child present or not. If the central figure was shown with a child, the child's age and gender were coded. The categories for child's age are infant, young child, teenager, and mix of ages. The categories for child's gender are boy, girl, both, and unknown (in the case of some infants).

Between 27 and 28% of men and women are shown with a spouse or partner (table not shown). Nevertheless, 29% of women are shown with children, compared to 19% of men. In addition, when the sample is restricted to those with children, there is a significant gender difference in the presence of a spouse or partner. While 62% of men with children also have a spouse or partner present, only 42% of women with children have a spouse or partner present.

Product Type

The categories for product type used in this study are "body" (health, hygiene, cleansing, or clothing), "car" (automobiles, auto accessories, and related products), "child" (diapers, baby food, children's medicine, or toys), "computers/electronics," "financial/insurance," "food," "home" (pertaining to home or housework), and "other." These categories are mutually exclusive. For example, most medications are included in the category for "body," but children's medicine is categorized as "child."

Setting

The categories for setting include "inside home," "outside at home" (yard/porch), and "away from home." These categories are mutually exclusive.

Housework Activities

Men's and women's participation in housework is one measure of their involvement with family and/or at home. The categories for housework include "cook/meal preparation," "wash dishes," "clean," "laundry," "shop," "yard work," and "auto/home maintenance." Each of these activities is coded as a binary variable so that a character can engage in any number of household tasks.

Activities with Children

In order to focus on involvement with children, a set of categories distinguishes between various activities. These categories include "child care" (e.g., taking care of sick children, changing diapers, or supervising children), "teach" (includes reading, teaching, or talking), "eat," and "play." Again, each of these activities is coded as a binary variable. Characters may participate in any or all of the four activities.

❧ Results

Analysis of Day Part

Table 1 shows gender differences in commercials by time, product type, and place for those with no children, those with children and spouse, and those with children but no spouse. Considering those with no children, women are more likely to appear in daytime commercials and less likely to appear in football commercials than men. Men are more likely to appear in football commercials than in commercials aired at other times. In contrast, only 11% of women appear during football commercials. Women are almost six times more likely to appear in commercials aired during daytime (63%). About one-quarter of women's and men's appearances occur during primetime.

If the sample is limited to those with spouses and children, the distribution of female characters across day parts remains similar to that for the sample of women without children. However, men with spouses and children resemble their wives and are more likely to appear in daytime commercials than men without children (61 versus 32%, respectively). In addition, only 13% of men with spouses and children appear in football commercials. Gender differences reemerge when we restrict the sample to those with children but no spouse. Similar to those without children, men with children but no spouse are more likely to appear in football commercials and less likely to appear in daytime commercials than their female counterparts.

TABLE 1 *Gender, Child, and Spouse Differences in Time, Product Type, and Place of Commercials*

| | No Children (%) | | Those with Children (%) | | | |
| | | | Spouse Present | | No Spouse Present | |
	Men	Women	Men	Women	Men	Women
Time						
Daytime	31.7	63.0*	60.7	60.7	50.0	72.5*
Primetime	26.0	26.1	26.8	26.8	17.7	20.0
Football	42.3	10.9*	12.5	12.5	32.4	7.5*
Product type						
Body	23.5	49.1*	7.1	7.1	5.9	13.8
Car	10.3	8.5	5.4	5.4	11.8	6.3
Child	0.0	0.3	7.1	7.1	14.7	28.8
Computer/ electronics	9.5	4.2*	5.4	5.4	17.7	1.3*
Financial/ insurance	3.9	2.1	5.4	5.4	2.9	0.0
Food	37.1	15.2*	50.0	50.0	29.4	27.5
Home	5.4	9.4*	10.7	10.7	0.0	8.8
Other	10.3	11.2	8.9	8.9	17.7	13.8
Place						
Inside home	18.0	33.9*	73.2	73.2	41.2	71.3*
Outside at home	2.8	4.6	5.4	5.4	14.7	3.8*
Away from home	79.1	61.5*	21.4	21.4	44.1	25.0*
(N)	(388)	(330)	(56)	(56)	(34)	(80)

*Difference between men and women significant at the .05 level.

Analysis of Products Advertised

There are also significant gender differences in the products advertised by women and men without children. Women without children are most likely to be shown in advertisements for body products (49%) and are more likely than men to advertise body products and home products. Men without children are most likely to appear in food commercials (37%) and are more likely than women to advertise food and computers and electronics.

When the sample is limited to those with children but no spouse, one gender difference remains significant. Only 1% of women with children but no spouse appear in commercials for computers and electronics compared to 18% of men with children but no spouse. A father and his teenage son are drawn closer by a satellite system in one commercial. Father and son used to do everything together but things change, until the father arrives home with a satellite dish. The son proceeds to help his father by handing him tools and reading directions. Other large (though not statistically significant) differences exist in who advertises body, car, child, and home products. For example, while 29% of women with children but no spouse appear in commercials for children's products, 15% of men with children but no spouse appear in these commercials. One commercial for children's vitamins asserts that "moms choose [brand]." This implies that fathers do not choose their children's vitamins.

Another product that is disproportionately aimed toward men is insurance. This is not immediately apparent in the numbers because many of these commercials are more subtle in their message for men, often through voice rather than appearance. Commercials for life insurance tend to depict men as financial providers and protectors of children. This is apparent in a commercial for health insurance in which a man sitting in a diner with a worried look questions, "What if something happens to my little girl?" In another commercial, three girls are running to school while a male voice says, "The more reasons you have for wanting the most secure life insurance, the better the quiet company sounds." The message is that men should provide for their children. Although no man is actually visible in the commercial, his security looms. He does not have to be there physically but must always be there financially.

Analysis of Setting

Both women and men without children are more likely to be shown away from home rather than inside their homes. However, women are more likely than men to appear at home while men are more likely than women to appear away from home. Yet the most likely setting for men and women with both spouse and children is inside the home rather than away from home. In general, when children are present, women and men are more likely to appear inside homes than when no children are present. However, gender differences widen among men and women with children but no spouse. A gender difference that had not emerged among other groups of men and women is the difference in how often men and women with children but no spouse appear outside at home. While this is the least likely location for both men and women, men with children but no spouse are twice as likely to appear outside at home as are women with children but no spouse.

Analysis of Housework

Housework is rarely performed in commercials by either women or men. Table 2 shows gender differences in housework. Cooking is the most prevalent task and is still performed by only 7% of women and 3% of men. However, women are more frequently shown performing housework. Women are significantly more likely to be shown cooking, cleaning, washing dishes, and shopping. If we consider how housework is divided, the evidence indicates that women perform the brunt of the work (data not shown). For example, 72% of the cooking was done by women compared to the 28% that men perform. Women are assumed to be in charge of cooking, especially when it involves holidays and entertaining guests. This may be subtle, as in a commercial for gelatin in which a woman says, "[This is] refreshing, like when my sister-in-law said this year we should have Thanksgiving at her house." This woman probably has a male relation (brother or brother-in-law) but yet does not refer to his house or him "having" Thanksgiving. Instead, the woman of the house is supposed to undertake this gathering of family. Men do not organize these events.

A common portrayal is that of the husband and children being waited on. Often a woman is contemplating what to make for dinner, and boxed dinners can act as a solution for women and hungry families. Another scenario is one in which the husband and children are not satisfied with the

TABLE 2 *Percentage of Men and Women Who Perform Household Tasks*

	Men	Women
Cook	2.7	7.3*
Wash dishes	0.2	3.0*
Clean	0.6	2.4*
Laundry	0.6	1.1
Shop	0.6	2.6*
Yard Work	0.6	0.6
Auto/home maintenance	0.4	0.4
(N)	(478)	(467)

*Difference between men and women significant at the .05 level.

food they are served. In these cases it is the woman's duty to please their families by cooking better food. One commercial has a husband attempting to cut tough porkchops and sarcastically thinking of a jackhammer. Another commercial asks, "Does cooking with less fat make your family less than enthusiastic?" With this prompt, a woman holding a casserole comes out of a kitchen and enters an empty dining room, with no sign of her family. Yet another commercial has a woman telephoning her female neighbor to tell her that she got the wrong parmesan cheese, while her husband, son, and mother/mother-in-law sit at the kitchen table waiting. All of these commercials are resolved when the wife gets the right product, and the outcome is a happy husband and children. The men in these commercials are not concerned with helping to improve the meals by cooking nor do they appear to be responsible for the products bought at the market. Instead, they are rather passive, just waiting to be served.

In place of an absent mother, a daughter may take over. This is the case in a commercial for cheese in which a daughter cooks dinner for the family because her mother is late at work. Again, the husband/father is passive, waiting to be served. In this case the traditional roles are being passed down from parents to children in that the brother is sitting with the father waiting for his sister to cook in place of the mother. This situation goes beyond the maintenance of traditional gender roles to the reproduction of these roles, creating a generational hierarchy within families.

The differences are even more dramatic for other household tasks. While about 79 to 80% of the cleaning and shopping in commercials was done by women, only 20 to 21% was done by men. One commercial has a mother endlessly food shopping and thinking about what she will feed her two growing teenage sons. The mother is shown in the kitchen, in a supermarket (with not one but two shopping carts full of food), and unloading bags of groceries from a car. Similarly, 93% of the dish washing was performed by women compared to only 7% by men. Men are often present but passive when their wives are performing household tasks. A woman cleans a carpet on her hands and knees while her husband, children, and mother/mother-in-law remain seated at the dining table in one commercial. Another commercial has women washing dishes while their husbands watch from behind.

When men are active within the household, it tends to be in activities considered male, such as taking the garbage out. Yet even when men participate in traditionally male household tasks, they are often shown to be incompetent. In one commercial, a man attempting to close a garbage bag is knocked over by a dog, which results in garbage being spilled all over the floor. His wife gives him the right brand of garbage bags so he can proceed to take out the garbage while his wife watches. This sex-based division of labor is traditional. The wife is knowledgeable about garbage bags yet does not actually take out the garbage herself. Rather, it is the husband's job. However, even when a wife is able to sit back and watch her husband do something, she often must guide him through the chore. The only activities performed equally by men and women were yard work and auto/home maintenance.

Analysis of Involvement with Children

Table 3 shows gender differences in child's age, child's gender, and involvement with children. Both men and women are more likely to be shown with young children than either infants or teenagers. However, men without

TABLE 3 *Gender Differences in Child's Age, Gender, and Activities (for Those with Children) by Presence of Spouse*

	Spouse Present		No Spouse Present	
	Men	Women	Men	Women
Child's age				
Infant	14.3	14.3	2.9	13.8*
Young	67.9	67.9	88.2	72.5*
Teen	10.7	10.7	8.8	12.5
Mix	7.1	7.1	0.0	1.3
Child's gender				
Boy(s)	25.0	25.0	47.1	30.0*
Girl(s)	7.1	7.1	47.1	41.3
Boy(s) and Girl(s)	58.9	58.9	5.9	21.3**
Unknown	8.9	8.9	0.0	7.5
Child activities				
Childcare	3.6	10.5	17.7	35.0*
Teach/read	17.9	1.8**	41.2	13.8**
Eat	44.6	42.1	11.8	1.3**
Play	25.0	21.1	52.9	27.5**
(N)	(56)	(56)	(34)	(80)

*Difference between men and women significant at the .10 level.

**Difference between men and women significant at the .05 level.

spouses are more likely to appear with young children and less likely to appear with infants than women without spouses. When a spouse is present, women and men are more likely to be shown with at least one child of each gender rather than only boys or only girls. However, when appearing alone with children, men are equally likely to appear with girls as with boys, while women are more likely to be shown with girls than with boys. This results in a significant difference in the presence of only boys. Men are more likely than women to be shown with only boys. On the other hand, women are more than three times more likely than men to appear with both girls and boys.

When comparing involvement with children among women and men with spouses, gender differences exist but reach significance only for teaching. Men are much more likely to be shown teaching or reading to a child than their wives. If we consider men and women who appear alone with children (i.e., no spouse), large gender differences emerge for all four activities. Women are more likely to be shown caring for children than doing any other activity with children. Men are more likely to be shown playing with or teaching a child than caring for a child. In fact, only 18% of men with children are shown caring for these children compared to 35% of women.

The concern of mothers for their children coupled with the absence of a father may be most obvious in commercials for children's medicine. A commercial for one brand claims that "mothers protect and care for the health and safety of their children in many different ways" and shows various mothers putting a life jacket on a son, a safety gate on a porch, a helmet on a daughter, and a son in a car seat. Several other commercials show mothers running after sneezing children, worrying about drowsy children, and hugging and kissing sick children. The message is that mothers take care of their

TABLE 4 *Percentage of Men and Women Involved in Child Activities (for Those with Children) by Age of Child*

	Men with			Women with		
	Infants	Children	Teenagers	Infants	Children	Teenagers
Child care	33.3	7.4	0.0	36.8	26.8	6.3
Teach/read	11.1	29.4	22.2	5.3	10.3	6.3
Eat	0.0	35.3	44.4	0.0	21.7	18.8
Play	55.6	36.8	22.2	57.9	21.7	12.5
(N)	(9)	(68)	(9)	(19)	(97)	(16)

children when they are sick. It should be noted that all of these commercials for children's medicines were run during daytime. The viewers are likely to be housewives who do take care of their children every day. The significance is probably not that fathers do not want the best for their children but that mothers are the ones who think about these things every day and must act to prevent injury or illness or in its event, to make their children better.

Instead, men are often shown teaching, reading, or talking to their child. While 41% of men read to or teach children, only 14% of women engage in these activities with children. This demonstrates the more instrumental role men play in their children's lives. In addition, a majority of men are shown playing with children, and men are significantly more likely to play than women. Men are also more likely to be shown eating with children than women.

The next stage in the analysis of involvement with children is to consider whether activities with children differ by child's age or gender. Table 4 shows the analysis of involvement by age of child, and Table 5 shows the analysis of involvement by gender of child. For men, the percentage who are shown caring for a child drops dramatically as children get older. One-third of men with infants are shown caring for those infants, while only 7% of men with young children are shown caring for them and no men are shown caring for teenagers. While the percentage of women shown caring for children also decreases with the child's age, the decline is not so dramatic. Over one-quarter of women with young children are shown caring for these children. There are also large gender differences in child care by the gender of the child. While 27% of men with boys are shown caring for the child, no men with girls are shown caring for the child. This can be compared to the 46% of women

TABLE 5 *Percentage of Men and Women Involved in Child Activities (for Those with Children) by Gender of Child*

	Men with			Women with		
	Boys	Girls	Both	Boys	Girls	Both
Child care	26.7	0.0	0.0	18.0	46.0	16.0
Teach/read	20.0	45.0	22.9	5.1	16.2	6.0
Eat	23.3	15.0	54.3	15.4	5.4	34.0
Play	36.7	50.0	22.9	12.8	29.7	16.0
(N)	(30)	(20)	(35)	(39)	(37)	(50)

shown caring for girls. In addition, only 18% of women are shown caring for boys, though 16% are shown caring for both girls and boys. In general, men are only shown caring for boys, while women are more likely to be shown caring for girls than boys. Nevertheless, child care is the most common activity for women when shown with girls, boys, or young children.

The patterns for teaching and reading to children are different from those shown for child care. For instance, teaching and reading are more likely to be performed with young children and teenagers than with infants. Another difference is that men are much more likely to read to or teach children than are women. For example, 29% of men teach or read to young children, compared to 10% of women. Finally, men are more likely to teach or read to female children than male children.

The general pattern for eating with children is that both men and women are more likely to be shown eating with young children or teenagers rather than with infants and are more likely to be shown eating with both girls and boys together rather than either gender alone. In fact, eating is the most common activity for men and women with teenagers and for those with both boys and girls.

However, playing is the most common activity for men with infants, young children, boys, or girls. The majority of both men and women with infants are shown playing with these infants (56 and 58%, respectively). Playing decreases with the child's age, but the decline is greater for women, which results in a significant gender difference in play with young children—37% of men, compared to 22% of women. There is also a significant gender difference in play with boys. While 37% of men play with boys, only 13% of women play with boys. Men are even more likely to play with girls than with boys.

● Summary and Discussion

The results of this study show that men's family roles are portrayed differently from women's family roles on television commercials. Several of the findings from this study are similar to those found in previous research. Men are more likely than women to appear in commercials aired during football. Men are also more likely to be shown away from home and less likely to be shown inside their home than women. Women are especially likely to be advertising "body" products, such as medication. Women are also more likely than men to be involved in domestic tasks, especially cooking, cleaning, washing dishes, and shopping.

Another finding consistent with previous research is that women are more likely than men to be shown with children and to be shown taking care of children. Consistent with Baruch and Barnett's (1983) finding that mothers spend more time alone with children than fathers, this study shows that the majority of women with children are pictured alone while the majority of men with children also have a spouse present. However, there are some further complexities in these results that go beyond previous research. One is that caregiving is a lot less common for men once their children are no longer infants. Child care is the least common activity for men with young children, while it is the most common activity for women with young children. Second, men are much less likely to care for female children than male children.

The most surprising finding may be that men are more likely to be involved in the three other child activities than women. It was expected that men would be more likely to play with children than be involved in other activities, but men are also more likely to teach or read to children and eat with children than women. The difference is especially dramatic for teaching and reading. Another unexpected finding is that men are more likely to teach, read, and play with female children than male children. It is unclear why this is the case, but it is important to keep in mind that men are more likely to be shown with male children than female children.

One of the activities that men are more likely to be involved in than women is eating. Commercials for breakfast and dessert foods and fast food restaurants are common. Mornings, especially weekend mornings, and late evenings may provide good opportunities for fathers to spend time with their children and take up some responsibilities for child care. In addition, fathers do not have to cook because these foods take little, if any, preparation. And fast food restaurants are increasingly crowded with fathers spending quality time with their children. Fast food establishments may specifically target fathers who work all week. One commercial has a boy who enters his parents' dark bedroom, tells his father to wake up, turns on the light, and shakes his sleeping father. The boys says, "It's Saturday, you said you would take me to [restaurant] for breakfast Saturday." The father puts on his glasses and replies, "I know." The son persists, "And you said I could have a [breakfast sandwich] and a big juice and you and mom would have pancakes and sausage and coffee and you said you wouldn't go to work today, you said." It is only 3:30 AM and the son is very anxious to spend time with his father. This commercial suggests that a father's time is rare but valuable.

However, a closer look at the products being advertised is informative. The message is that fathers can be involved without spending much time doing daily child care tasks. The most nutritious foods in these commercials are cereals; other than cereal, the food is more for fun than for nutrition. Other products advertised in nontraditional ways, such as insurance and cars, are still traditionally in the realm of the male. Men are expected to provide for their families and look out for the safety of their children. From these commercials, we see that Bernard's (1981) image of the "good provider" is still well intact. Finally, sports and technical knowledge are also stereotypically in the domain of men, and technology and toys are items that men like to play with, too. One commercial has a father playing with his son's racetrack while another commercial has a father showing his children how to play softball. Sometimes the fathers are so interested in playing that they forget their children want to play, as in a commercial for a computer in which a father is supposed to be teaching his son how to use the computer. The father becomes so engrossed with the computer that his son tries jumping up and down in an attempt to attract his father's attention away from the computer. In fact, research by Hochschild (1989) and Parke and Stearns (1993) shows that much of the time fathers spend with their children is in play activities. This is a way for many fathers to be good, responsible fathers without doing the "dirty work" or daily caretaking. It may even shape a new form of domestic involvement, that of playmate.

While some previous studies suggest a faster change in men's image than behavior, results from this study suggest that even images are slow to change. The image of men in most commercials, especially daytime commercials, is not one of involved husband and father. Contrary to the finding by Lamb and colleagues (1982) that real fathers are as competent as mothers, husbands and fathers in commercials are, for the most part, passive, incompetent, or dependent on their wives. The image of the involved family man presents itself in few commercials. The father baking cookies is literally 1 in 1000. The expansion of fathers' roles in commercials to include more nontraditional roles may, in some ways, still be traditional. While they appear to be involved family men, the men portrayed often rely on products that appeal to traditional men. When we take into account the actual products being advertised, we see that only certain product types can sustain male involvement, and these product types lend themselves to traditional men. Those that are involved need not know how to cook or clean or care for a sick child. Instead, their knowledge of traditionally male products is sufficient. These images are important given their extensiveness and potential to influence attitudes. Commercials may act as a socializing agent for parents, especially for fathers. In a time when men's roles are changing, real men need a point of comparison. They cannot look to their own fathers. This leaves friends and neighbors and cultural images, including those 30-second spots that break up our favorite television shows and sports events. If this is the case, real husbands and fathers may look to the images of husbands and fathers for their daily lessons on what, when, where, and how much is expected.

Future research should continue to monitor the image of men as husbands and fathers in television commercials and the media more generally. Studies that consider men's changing image will be especially important. In this regard, the next step would be to obtain longitudinal data. Another direction for further research is to consider the influence of television on adult men. Are men making comparisons, directly or indirectly, to the images they see on television? More needs to be done to investigate the influence of media on gender role attitudes and child care behaviors of men.

References

Atkinson, M. P., and Blackwelder, S. P. (1993). Fathering in the 20th century. *Journal of Marriage and the Family, 55,* 975–986.

Baruch, G., and Barnett, R. C. (1983). Adult daughters' relationships with their mothers. *Journal of Marriage and the Family, 45,* 601–606.

Berk, S. F. (1985). *The gender factory: The apportionment of work in American households.* New York: Plenum.

Bernard, J. (1981). The good-provider role: Its rise and fall. *American Psychologist, 36,* 1–12.

Blakeney, M., Barnes, S., and McKeough, J. (1983). Gender advertising: The self-fulfilling prophecy? *Australian Journal of Social Issues, 18,* 171–181.

Boulton, M. G. (1983). *On being a mother: A study of women with pre-school children.* London: Tavistock.

Bretl, D. J., and Cantor, J. (1988). The portrayal of men and women in U.S. television commercials: A recent content analysis and trends over 15 years. *Sex Roles, 18,* 595–609.

Cherlin, A. (1992). *Marriage, divorce, remarriage,* Cambridge, MA: Harvard University Press.

Coltrane, S., and Allan, K. (1994). "New" fathers and old stereotypes: Representations of masculinity in 1980 television advertising. *Masculinities, 2,* 43–66.

Craig, R. S. (1992a). Women as home caregivers: Gender portrayal in OTC drug commercials. *Journal of Drug Education, 22,* 303–312.

Craig, R. S. (1992b). The effect of television day part on gender portrayals in television commercials: A content analysis. *Sex Roles, 26,* 197–211.

Demo, D. H., and Acock, A. C. (1993). Family diversity and the division of domestic labor: How much have things really changed? *Family Relations, 42,* 323–331.

Furnham, A., and Schofield, S. (1986). Sex-role stereotyping in British radio advertisements. *British Journal of Social Psychology, 25,* 165–171.

Garst, J., and Bodenhausen, G. V. (1997). Advertising's effects on men's gender role attitudes. *Sex Roles, 36,* 551–572.

Gershuny, J., and Robinson, J. P. (1988). Historical changes in the household division of labor. *Demography, 25,* 537–554.

Goldscheider, F. K., and Waite, L. J. (1991). *New families, no families? The transformation of the American home.* Berkeley: University of California Press.

Hochschild, A., with Machung, A. (1989). *The second shift: Working parents and the revolution at home.* New York: Viking.

Huang, J. H. (1995). National character and sex roles in advertising. *Journal of International Consumer Marketing, 7,* 81–96.

Kellner, D. (1990). *Television and the crisis of democracy.* Boulder, CO: Westview.

Kimball, M. M. (1986). Television and sex-role attitudes. In T. M. Williams (Ed.) *The impact of television: A natural experiment in three communities* (pp. 265–301). London: Academic Press.

Krippendorff, K. (1980). *Content analysis: An introduction to its methodology.* Beverly Hills, CA: Sage.

Lamb, M. E., Frodi, A. M., Hwang, C.-P., and Frodi, M. (1982). Varying degrees of paternal involvement in infant care: Attitudinal and behavioral correlates. In M. E. Lamb (Ed.), *Non-traditional families: Parenting and child development* (pp. 117–137). Hillsdale, NJ: Lawrence Erlbaum.

LaRossa, R. (1988). Fatherhood and social change. *Family Relations, 37,* 451–457.

Levitan, S. A., Belous, R. S., and Gallo, F. (1988). *What's happening to the American family?* Baltimore: John Hopkins University Press.

Lewis, C. (1986). *Becoming a father.* Milton Keynes, England: Open University Press.

Lovdal, L. T. (1989). Sex role messages in television commercials: An update. *Sex Roles, 21,* 715–724.

Manstead, A. S. R., and McCulloch, C. (1981). Sex-role stereotyping in British television advertisements. *British Journal of Social Psychology, 20,* 171–180.

Mazzella, C., Durkin, K., Cerini, E., and Buralli, P. (1992). Sex role stereotyping in Australian television advertisements. *Sex Roles, 26,* 243–259.

Messner, M. A. (1993). "Changing men" and feminist politics in the United States. *Theory and Society, 22,* 723–738.

O'Bryant, S. L., and Corder-Bolz, C. R. (1978). The effects of television on children's stereotyping of women's work roles. *Journal of Vocational Behavior, 12,* 233–244.

Parke, R. D., and Stearns, P. N. (1993). Fathers and child rearing. In G. H. Elder, J. Modell, and R. D. Parke (Eds.), *Children in time and place* (pp. 147–170). Cambridge: Cambridge University Press.

Perimenis, L. (1991). The ritual of anorexia nervosa in cultural context. *Journal of American Culture, 14,* 49–59.

Pleck, J. H. (1987). American fathering in historical perspective. In M. Kimmel (Ed.), *Changing men* (pp. 83–97). Newbury Park, CA: Sage.

Pollner, M. (1982). Better dead than wed. *Social Policy, 13,* 28–31.

Riffe, D., Place, P. C., and Mayo, C. M. (1993). Game time, soap time and prime time TV ads: Treatment of women in Sunday football and rest-of-week advertising. *Journalism Quarterly, 70,* 437–446.

Ross, C. E., Mirowsky, J., and Huber, J. (1983). Dividing work, sharing work, and in-between: Marriage patterns and depression. *American Sociological Review, 48,* 809–823.

Rossi, A. S. (1984). Gender and parenthood. *American Sociological Review, 49,* 1–19.

Signorielli, N. (1990). Children, television, and gender roles: Messages and impact. *Journal of Adolescent Health Care, 11,* 50–58.

Signorelli, N. (1991). *A sourcebook on children and television.* New York: Greenwood Press.

Tan, A. S. (1979). TV beauty adds and role expectations of adolescent female viewers. *Journalism Quarterly, 56,* 283–288.

Thompson, L., and Walker, A. J. (1989). Gender in families. *Journal of Marriage and the Family, 51,* 845–871.

U.S. Bureau of the Census. (1995). *Statistical abstract of the United States: 1995* (115th ed.). Washington, DC: U.S. Government Printing Office.

Veroff, J., Douvan, E., and Kulka, R. A. (1981). *The inner American: A self-portrait from 1957 to 1976.* New York: Basic Books.

☻ ☻ ☻

Questions

1. According to the author, what is the relationship between television viewing habits and gender attitudes?

2. Briefly describe how men and women are portrayed doing housework in commercials in this article. How closely do these findings match your own life experiences? Explain.

3. Summarize Kaufman's findings about how relationships between men and children are portrayed in commercials. How does this compare to the way women and children are portrayed?

4. Expand Kaufman's research, and examine the family roles women and men play in print advertisements. Select two magazines and record what you see by using the categories devised by Kaufman. What are your findings? How do they compare to Kaufman's?

Love, American Style

LISA E. PHILLIPS

Are you married? Do you ever plan to marry? Are your parents still married to one another? This article examines marriage patterns, divorce rates, and living arrangements in the United States over two generations: "boomers" and "Generation Xers."

*L*ove is in the air, but marriage must be in the water. How else to explain Americans' attraction to matrimony? According to "Marital Status and Living Arrangements: March 1998," a recently updated U.S. Census Bureau report released last month, about 56% of all American adults were married and living with their spouses last year (111 million people). Not surprisingly, California, Texas, New York, Florida, and Nevada were the top five states, respectively, for marriages in 1996.

That's a pretty rosy picture of family values, even taking into consideration the downside of the report: that about 10% of adults (19.4 million) were "currently divorced" last year. It's the word *currently* that defines us: Hope springs eternal. Divorce isn't forever.

"People aspire to what they don't have," says Steve Kraus, a director at Yankelovich Partners, explaining the behavior patterns of boomers who are marrying, divorcing, and remarrying, versus Generation Xers, many of whom are holding off on making that big commitment for the first time "Not every Gen Xer is a child of divorce," he adds, "But the 1980s were their formative years, when divorce rates sky rocketed."

That's why, according to a recently released Yankelovich poll, Gen Xers—the half that aren't already hitched—are delaying marriage, as

---

"Love, American Style," by Lisa E. Phillips, reprinted from *American Demographics*, Vol. 21, 1999. pp. 56–56.

Gen X Marriages in Y2K+

Marital status, projections by age for years 2000 and 2010				
Characteristic	# (000s)		Percent distribution	
	2000	2010	2000	2010
Total population 18+	203,852	225,206	100%	100%
Never married/single	44,459	50,747	21.8%	22.5%
Married at least once	159,393	174,459	78.2%	77.5%
Population 25–34 years	37,233	38,521	100%	100%
Never married/single	12,288	5,660	33.0%	14.7%
Married at least once	24,946	32,860	67.0%	85.3%
Population, 35–54 years	81,689	78,847	100%	100%
Never married/single	8,232	4,741	10.1%	6.0%
Married at least once	73,458	74,108	89.9%	94.0%

Source: Census Bureau, *Current Population Reports*, p. 25–1129, and *American Demographics*.

In general, Generation X is putting off marriage—at least for another decade, according to current Census Bureau projections. Boomers, on the other hand, are taking the plunge—some over and over again.

shown by the current median age at the time of first marriage: 25 years for women and 26.8 years for men in 1997. Boomers, by contrast, were marrying young: In 1970, the median age for marriage for women was 20.8 years, and for men, 23.2 years.

Yankelovich's survey of some 2,500 Gen Xers shows that those who are still single are planning to enjoy themselves, while those who are married are nesting with a vengeance. Fifty-eight percent of single Xers say their social life is a high priority, compared to only 38% of married Xers. Some 61% of singles feel it's vital to keep up on media trends, compared to 49% of their married friends. And when it comes to fun, 68% of single Xers expect to have "more fun" this year, while a mere 52% of married people are counting on it.

Kirsty Doig, vice president of New York City-based Youth Intelligence, hasn't found that attitude among the Gen Xers she's spo-

Virginia is for Lovers

Counties where single population is greater than the married population

Name	State	Single	Married	Ratio (S/M)
1) Williamsburg City	VA	6,721	2,645	2.54
2) Radford City	VA	8,568	4,222	2.03
3) Lexington City	VA	3,425	1,963	1.74
4) District of Columbia	DC	242,035	146,213	1.66
5) Harrisonburg City	VA	13,712	9,196	1.49
6) Claiborne	MS	4,242	2,877	1.47
7) Suffolk	MA	270,440	185,906	1.45
8) Shannon	SD	2,830	2,048	1.38
9) New York	NY	571,206	435,595	1.31
10) Clarke	GA	35,051	27,183	1.29

Source: 1990 Census, CACI

Virginia and neighboring Washington, D.C., take the country's top-five places for number of singles-to-married couples. However, college kids at William and Mary, not to mention Georgetown, George Washington University, and the Catholic University of America, make up a great deal of the single population in Williamsburg and Washington, while Clarke County, Georgia, is home to the University of Georgia.

ken to. "They don't feel they lose their identity by getting married, and they're not looking at marriage as an end to their fun," she says.

Gen Xers, she adds, felt abandoned as they grew up. "They were latch-key kids, many were the children of divorce, and the media told them they were stupid," Doig says. "So they turned to their peers for support."

Nationally, there is nearly one divorce for every two marriages, according to census data from 1996, the most current year available. Preliminary figures from the *Monthly Vital Statistics Report* for the first seven months of 1998 don't indicate a major shift in that trend.

But on average, Americans are staying married longer. The median duration of marriages ending in divorce has lengthened—from 6.7 years in 1970 to 7.2 years in 1990, according to the U.S. National Center for Health Statistics.

And we're older when we finally call it quits. The median age at divorce for men was 35.9 years in 1990, or 2.7 years older than in 1970. Women's median age at the time of their divorce in 1990 was 33.2, up 3.4 years from 1970.

The rate of remarriage has slowed, as well. In 1970, 12.3% of divorced women and 20.5% of divorced men remarried. By 1990, just 7.6% of divorced women and 10.6% of divorced men were heading back to the altar.

Still, the Census Bureau is predicting an upswing in Gen X marriages by 2010. About half of them are married now, and census projections indicate about two-thirds will be hitched by 2001, when the true millennium rolls around. By 2010, 83% will be settling down.

☙ Tradition with a Twist

But settling down to what? Traditional family values, on their own term. Something edgier, with more irony than their parents. "They want to do traditional family things, like spend time on the family photo album," Kraus notes. "But instead of putting the pictures in a book, they'll scan them into their computers and put them on a Web site."

Youth Intelligence's Doig agrees. "Marriage isn't a locked jail to Gen Xers," she says. "They may not be more committed to it than their parents, but they're redefining it for themselves." If, for example, Gen Xers wish to stay at home with their children, they'll find ways to telecommute or jobs that will allow them to share the responsibility.

Both Doig and Kraus use the word *nostalgic* to describe Xers' view of hearth and home. The Xers, though, are nostalgic for the childhood that boomers supposedly had. It's informed their model for the perfect, traditional marriage.

"The stereotypical boomer grew up watching *Leave It To Beaver*," says Kraus. "The stereotypical Gen Xer grew up watching *The Brady Bunch*. Their impression of family life was, 'Hey, let's go find a bunch of strangers to live with us.'" It's a wonder they want to get married at all. . . .

☻ ☻ ☻

Questions

1. How do the marriage patterns of boomers differ from those of Gen Xers?

2. How do Gen Xers view marriage? Why do they view it that way? If you are a Gen Xer, are the view points discussed in this article consistent with how you see marriage?

3. Go to the library (or use the Internet) to locate data on marriage rates in two countries. Are people in these countries as "marriage-minded" as Americans? Explain.

4. Ask ten students on your campus whether they intend to get married. If they do, ask them why. (If some of them are already married, ask why they married.) If they do not intend to marry, invite them to explain their reasons. Pool your data with information collected by your classmates. What did you learn about students' marital intentions?

The Way We Weren't: The Myth and Reality of the "Traditional" Family

STEPHANIE COONTZ

Many politicians and religious leaders have urged a return to the "traditional" family. However, historian Stephanie Coontz argues that this supposed "traditional" family is actually mythological. In this article, she provides snapshots of family life from colonial to present times. By doing so, she reveals that none of these family structures protected people from inequalities based on race, class, gender, or interpersonal conflict.

. . .

Colonial Families

American families always have been diverse, and the male breadwinner-female homemaker, nuclear ideal that most people associate with "the" traditional family has predominated for only a small portion of our history. In colonial America, several types of families coexisted or competed. Native American kinship systems subordinated the nuclear family to a much larger network of marital alliances and kin obligations, ensuring that no single family was forced to go it alone.

Wealthy settler families from Europe, by contrast, formed independent households that pulled in labor from poorer neighbors and relatives, building their extended family solidarities on the backs of truncated families among indentured servants, slaves, and the poor. Even wealthy families, though, often were disrupted by death; a majority of colonial Americans probably spent some time in a step-family. Meanwhile, African Americans, denied the legal protection of marriage and parenthood, built extensive kinship networks and obligations through fictive kin ties, ritual co-parenting or godparenting, adoption of orphans, and complex naming patterns designed to preserve family links across space and time.

The dominant family values of colonial days left no room for sentimentalizing childhood. Colonial mothers, for example, spent far less time doing child care than do modern working women, typically delegating this task to servants or older siblings. Among white families, patriarchal authority was so absolute that disobedience by wife or child was seen as a small form of treason, theoretically punishable by death, and family relations were based on power, not love.

❧ The Nineteenth-Century Family

With the emergence of a wage-labor system and a national market in the first third of the nineteenth century, white middle-class families became less patriarchal and more child-centered. The ideal of the male breadwinner and the nurturing mother now appeared. But the emergence of domesticity for middle-class women and children depended on its absence among the immigrant, working class, and African American women or children who worked as servants, grew the cotton, or toiled in the textile mills to free middle-class wives from the chores that had occupied their time previously.

Even in the minority of nineteenth-century families who could afford domesticity, though, emotional arrangements were quite different from nostalgic images of "traditional" families. Rigid insistence on separate spheres for men and women made male-female relations extremely stilted, so that women commonly turned to other women, not their husbands, for their most intimate relations. The idea that all of one's passionate feelings should go toward a member of the opposite sex was a twentieth-century invention—closely associated with the emergence of a mass consumer society and promulgated by the very film industry that "traditionalists" now blame for undermining such values.

❂ Early Twentieth-Century Families

Throughout the nineteenth century, at least as much divergence and disruption in the experience of family life existed as does today, even though divorce and unwed motherhood were less common. Indeed, couples who marry today have a better chance of celebrating a fortieth wedding anniversary than at any previous time in history. The life cycles of nineteenth-century youth (in job entry, completion of schooling, age at marriage, and establishment of separate residence) were far more diverse than they became in the early twentieth-century. At the turn of the century a higher proportion of people remained single for their entire lives than at any period since. Not until the 1920s did a bare majority of children come to live in a male breadwinner-female homemaker family, and even at the height of this family form in the 1950s, only 60% of American children spent their entire childhoods in such a family.

From about 1900 to the 1920s, the growth of mass production and emergence of a public policy aimed at establishing a family wage led to new ideas about family self-sufficiency, especially in the white middle class and a privileged sector of the working class. The resulting families lost their organic connection to intermediary units in society such as local shops, neighborhood work cultures and churches, ethnic associations, and mutual-aid organizations.

As families related more directly to the state, the market, and the mass media, they also developed a new cult of privacy, along with heightened expectations about the family's role in fostering individual fulfillment. New family values stressed the early independence of children and the romantic coupling of husband and wife, repudiating the intense same-sex ties and mother-infant bonding of earlier years as unhealthy. From this family we get the idea that women are sexual, that youth is attractive, and that marriage should be the center of our emotional fulfillment.

Even aside from its lack of relevance to the lives of most immigrants, Mexican Americans, African Americans, rural families, and the urban poor, big contradictions existed between image and reality in the middle-class family ideal of the early twentieth century. This is the period when many Americans first accepted the idea that the family should be sacred from outside intervention; yet the development of the private, self-sufficient family depended on state intervention in the economy, government regulation of parent-child relations, and state-directed destruction of class and community institutions that hindered the development of family privacy. Acceptance of a youth and leisure culture sanctioned early marriage and raised expectations about the quality of married life, but also introduced new tensions between the generations and new conflicts between husband and wife over what were adequate levels of financial and emotional support.

The nineteenth-century middle-class ideal of the family as a refuge from the world of work was surprisingly modest compared with emerging twentieth-century demands that the family provide a whole alternative world of satisfaction and intimacy to that of work and neighborhood. Where a family succeeded in doing so, people might find pleasures in the home never before imagined. But the new ideals also increased the possibilities for failure: America has had the highest divorce rate in the world since the turn of the century.

In the 1920s, these contradictions created a sense of foreboding about "the future of the family" that was every bit as widespread and intense as today's. Social scientists and popular commentators of the time hearkened back to the "good old days," bemoaning the sexual revolution, the fragility of nuclear family ties, the cult of youthful romance, the decline of respect for grandparents, and the threat of the

"New Woman." But such criticism was sidetracked by the stock-market crash, the Great Depression of the 1930s, and the advent of World War II.

Domestic violence escalated during the Depression, while murder rates were as high in the 1930s as in the 1980s. Divorce rates fell, but desertion increased and fertility plummeted. The war stimulated a marriage boom, but by the late 1940s one in every three marriages was ending in divorce.

❀ The 1950s Family

At the end of the 1940s, after the hardships of the Depression and war, many Americans revived the nuclear family ideals that had so disturbed commentators during the 1920s. The unprecedented post-war prosperity allowed young families to achieve consumer satisfactions and socioeconomic mobility that would have been inconceivable in earlier days. The 1950s family that resulted from these economic and cultural trends, however, was hardly "traditional." Indeed it is best seen as a historical aberration. For the first time in 100 years, divorce rates dropped, fertility soared, the gap between men's and women's job and educational prospects widened (making middle-class women more dependent on marriage), and the age of marriage fell—to the point that teenage birth rates were almost double what they are today.

Admirers of these very *nontraditional* 1950s family forms and values point out that household arrangements and gender roles were less diverse in the 1950s than today, and marriages more stable. But this was partly because diversity was ruthlessly suppressed and partly because economic and political support systems for socially-sanctioned families were far more generous than they are today. Real wages rose more in any single year of the 1950s than they did in the entire decade of the 1980s; the average thirty-year-old man could buy a median-priced home on 15 to 18% of his income. The government funded public investment, home ownership, and job creation at a rate more than triple that of the past two decades, while 40% of young men were eligible for veteran's benefits. Forming and maintaining families was far easier than it is today.

Yet the stability of these 1950s families did not guarantee good outcomes for their members. Even though most births occurred within wedlock, almost a third of American children lived in poverty during the 1950s, a higher figure than today. More than 50% of black married-couple families were poor. Women were often refused the right to serve on juries, sign contracts, take out credit cards in their own names, or establish legal residence. Wife-battering rates were low, but that was because wife-beating was seldom counted as a crime. Most victims of incest, such as Miss America of 1958, kept the secret of their fathers' abuse until the 1970s or 1980s, when the women's movement became powerful enough to offer them the support denied them in the 1950s.

◉ The Post-1950s Family

In the 1960s, the civil rights, antiwar, and women's liberation movements exposed the racial, economic, and sexual injustices that had been papered over by the Ozzie and Harriet images on television. Their activism made older kinds of public and private oppression unacceptable and helped create the incomplete, flawed, but much-needed reforms of the Great Society. Contrary to the big lie of the past decade that such programs caused our current family dilemmas, those antipoverty and social justice reforms helped overcome many of the family problems that prevailed in the 1950s.

In 1964, after 14 years of unrivaled family stability and economic prosperity, the poverty rate was still 19%; in 1969, after five years of civil rights activism, the rebirth of feminism, and the institution of nontraditional if relatively modest government welfare programs, it was down to 12%, a low that has not been seen again since the social welfare cutbacks began in the late 1970s. In 1965, 20% of American children still lived in poverty; within five years, that had fallen to 15%. Infant mortality was cut in half between 1965 and 1980. The gap in nutrition between low-income Americans and other

Americans narrowed significantly, as a direct result of food stamp and school lunch programs. In 1963, 20% of Americans living below the poverty line had *never* been examined by a physician; by 1970 this was true of only 8% of the poor.

Since 1973, however, real wages have been falling for most Americans. Attempts to counter this through tax revolts and spending freezes have led to drastic cutbacks in government investment programs. Corporations also spend far less on research and job creation than they did in the 1950s and 1960s, though the average compensation to executives has soared. The gap between rich and poor, according to the April 17, 1995, *New York Times,* is higher in the United States than in any other industrial nation.

◉ Family Stress

These inequities are not driven by changes in family forms, contrary to ideologues who persist in confusing correlations with causes; but they certainly exacerbate such changes, and they tend to bring out the worst in *all* families. The result has been an accumulation of stresses on families, alongside some important expansions of personal options. Working couples with children try to balance three full-time jobs, as employers and schools cling to policies that assume every employee has a "wife" at home to take care of family matters. Divorce and remarriage have allowed many adults and children to escape from toxic family environments, yet our lack of social support networks and failure to forge new values for sustaining intergenerational obligations have let many children fall through the cracks in the process.

Meanwhile, young people find it harder and harder to form or sustain families. According to an Associated Press report of April 25, 1995, the median income of men aged 25 to 34 fell by 26% between 1972 and 1994, while the proportion of such men with earnings below the poverty level for a family of four more than doubled to 32%. The figures are even worse for African American and Latino men. Poor individuals are twice as likely to divorce as more affluent ones, three to four times less likely to marry in the first place, and five to seven times more likely to have a child out of wedlock.

As conservatives insist, there is a moral crisis as well as an economic one in modern America: a pervasive sense of social alienation, new levels of violence, and a decreasing willingness to make sacrifices for others. But romanticizing "traditional" families and gender roles will not produce the changes in job structures, work policies, child care, medical practice, educational preparation, political discourse, and gender inequities that would permit families to develop moral and ethical systems relevant to 1990s realities.

America needs more than a revival of the narrow family obligations of the 1950s, whose (greatly exaggerated) protection for white, middle-class children was achieved only at tremendous cost to the women in those families and to all those who could not or would not aspire to the Ozzie and Harriet ideal. We need a concern for children that goes beyond the question of whether a mother is waiting with cookies when her kids come home from school. We need a moral language that allows us to address something besides people's sexual habits. We need to build values and social institutions that can reconcile people's needs for independence with their equally important rights to dependence, and surely we must reject older solutions that involved balancing these needs on the backs of women. We will not find our answers in nostalgia for a mythical "traditional family."

☺ ☺ ☺

Questions

1. Describe how children and childhood were perceived in colonial times. How does this perception compare to our view of children today? What changes in society caused us to change our perspective?

2. If you were a white female, in which historical period would you choose to live? Which historical period would you select if you were African American? Explain why you made these choices.

3. According to Coontz, what puts stress on families today? What can we do to relieve some of this stress?

4. Suppose that an editorial appearing in your local newspaper called for a return to the traditional family values of the 1950s as a way to save the family. Write a letter to the editor explaining why this plea is neither feasible nor desirable.

Diverse Forms of Family Life Merit Recognition

ROSEMARY RADFORD RUETHER

What is a family? Many Americans might say that a family consists of a man, a woman, and their children. However, as theologian Rosemary Radford Ruether notes, this "traditional family" constitutes only about 25 percent of all U.S. households. In this essay, Ruether makes a case for expanding our definition of family. She argues that the phrase "family values" implies an ideological bias toward just one form of family—one that no longer works for most Americans and that harms poor families.

Support for the many ways people pledge fidelity is a step to better family policy.

American families are increasingly diverse in their forms. It is no longer possible to speak of one normative form of the family in relation to which all others are regarded as deviant. According to the 1996 census, there were 100 million households in the United States, a full 30 million of which consist of single people, men or women. These single-person householders are people across all stages of the life cycle, from unmarried young professionals, never married or divorced middle-aged men or women, and older men or women. Thus the single-person household has become one of the major forms of the U.S. household.

The largest type of household is the two-earner married couple, with or without dependents. This type of household accounts for about 34 percent of households.

The married couple with only the male as breadwinner, or what some see as the "traditional family," is now only about 22 million households, or less than a fourth of all households. Female-headed households with dependents are about 13 percent of households, and male-headed households with dependents and no spouse are about 3 percent. These bare statistics conceal much more diversity. Gay and lesbian couples with or without children or other dependents may be around 5 percent of households, although they are listed as single persons or male- or female-headed households.

About half of American marriages end in divorce and about 80 percent of those remarry, so many households consist of blended families. Americans are marrying later, in their late 20s or early 30s, especially for those men and women establishing a professional career, and these professional women are having babies later than any time in history, in their 30s and even early 40s.

This diversity is causing consternation to those social conservatives who assume that there is only one form of family divinely mandated by God, and that is the patriarchal heterosexual family with working male breadwinner and dependent wife. But contrary to the rhetoric of Christian social conservatives, this form of the family is not to be found in the Bible and was only a minority expression of the family for the white middle class in the late 19th to mid-20th centuries.

Many forms of family are found in Hebrew scripture, one of the most typical being the polygamous family, usually with two wives, the children of both wives and also servants or slaves and their children. The New Testament is distinguished by a sharp attack on the patriarchal slaveholding family in favor of a vision of a new age in which "there will be no more marrying and giving in marriage." In the later strata of the New Testament in the post-Pauline epistles, there was an effort to restore the patriarchal slaveholding family as normative for Christians, but this was contested by those who clung to the anti-family tradition.

Through most of human history, husband, wife and their children have worked together in household economies. The split between home and work, as separate female and male spheres, arose only with the white management class after industrialization. It is this group that created the ideology of the dependent unemployed wife or "full-time housewife," but this ideal was inaccessible for most working class, black and immigrant families who depended on the wages of both husband and wife and also those of older children.

The possibility of a wife who is not employed depends on a male wage sufficient by itself to support the whole family comfortably. Most white middle-class people no longer see themselves as having an adequate income from one breadwinner and depend on at least two workers in a family for an adequate wage. Thus the predominance of the two-earner household is the result less of feminism than of economics, although feminism has played a major role in giving women access to civil rights, education and better-paid jobs.

Although they are only a few percent of American households, gay and lesbian couples have become a major flash point of controversy in American society precisely because they are seeking normalization of their status as families with the same legal rights as heterosexual families. Legal marriage in the United States carries with it a package of benefits: the right to share medical benefits, inherit a pension, parental rights toward children and the like, all of which are denied to gay and lesbian couples.

An increasing number of gay men and lesbians are raising children, either children from a former heterosexual marriage, adopted children or children created through artificial insemination. Some lesbian couples are choosing to have one spouse bear one child and the other spouse bear the next, sometimes with semen donated by the same male so the children will be related. Lesbians are asking for the legal right for the partner who did not give birth to adopt the child borne by the other partner, something at present allowed by only a few states.

Vermont is the first state to pass a law that allows full and equal civil legal status to gay and lesbian couples. Despite the uproar over this, I suspect it will become more common in the United States, as is already the case in Europe, because it is a reform that favors responsible relationships of couples toward each other and toward dependents. That is in the interests of society.

What has been called "family values" by the Christian right is basically an ideological insistence on one form of family that no longer works for most Americans, and that actually results in the impoverishment of the poorest families by denying such basic needs as better wages, adequate health care and child care. A better family policy for both the churches and society involves acceptance of and support for a diversity of family forms. This diversity is already the reality of American life. We need to help people in these diverse forms of households be as well housed—with adequate pay, medical care and education—as possible, supporting the many ways people are pledging fidelity and commitment to the well-being of one another.

The values of mutuality and commitment to each other are not lessened but expanded when they are affirmed in the many forms that households and committed relationships actually exist in people's lives. We need to unmask the rhetoric that insists that affirmation of civil marriage and church blessings of "holy unions" somehow demeans marriage for heterosexuals. All our unions are made holier by expanding the opportunities for faithful relationship, joyful blessing and legal responsibility between all people.

❧ ❧ ❧

Questions

1. Briefly summarize Ruether's argument about family. Do you agree or disagree with her perspective? Explain your views.

2. Why does family diversity upset Christian social conservatives? Why does the author say that this concern is misplaced?

3. Explain why gay and lesbian families are a "flashpoint of controversy" in the United States.

4. Why does Ruether argue that "family values" are harmful? To whom are they harmful, and in what ways?

5. Ask 10 students who are not in your class whether they would support an initiative like the one passed in Vermont which gives full and equal legal status to gay and lesbian couples. Ask why they would or would not support such an initiative. Compare your results to those of your classmates'. What did you learn?

A Comparison of Marriages and Cohabiting Relationships

STEVEN L. NOCK

University of Virginia

Are married people different in important ways from people who cohabit, or live together? Steven Nock researched this question and discovered that there were differences in levels of commitment and happiness between cohabiting and married couples. In the article below, Nock argues that these differences might stem from a self-selection process rather than marital status.

☺ Introduction

There were over 3 million unmarried cohabiting couples in America in 1991, half a million more than in 1988 (U.S. Bureau of the Census, 1989, 1992). The increase in nonmarital cohabitation has been rapid and sustained for two decades, prompting social scientists to speculate about the implications of this trend for the institution of marriage.

Although we know more about cohabiting unions now than we did 10 years ago, one central question remains largely unexplored. Specifically, we know little about how individuals and couples differ

---

"A Comparison of Marriages and Cohabitating Relationships," by Steven L. Nock, reprinted from *Journal of Family Issues*, Vol. 16, 1995. pp. 53–76.

in terms of the nature and quality of their relationships. This article addresses that issue by examining various dimensions of relationships of married and cohabiting individuals predicted to differ because of basic sociological processes.

Cohabitation is an increasingly common prelude to marriage. By their early 30s, almost one half of the U.S. population has cohabited at some time. The majority of marriages begun since 1985 began as cohabitation (Bumpass & Sweet, 1989). As an element of "mate-selection," cohabitation is probably at least as commonplace today as going steady was 30 years ago.

Cohabitation is also gaining popularity as an alternative to marriage—especially for those who have already been married and divorced. Of all cohabiting unions in 1991, only one third (30%) involved two never-married adults whereas almost all others (69%) included at least one divorced person (U.S. Bureau of the Census, 1992, Table 8). Most divorced individuals will eventually remarry. However, time spent in a cohabiting relationship delays remarriage just as it does first marriage; that is, it is an alternative to marriage or remarriage even if temporary (see Sweet & Bumpass, 1987, on first marriage).

There are good reasons to suspect that the relationships of married and cohabiting couples differ in important ways. We know, for example, that people who cohabit prior to marriage have considerably higher divorce rates regardless of whether they marry their cohabiting partner or someone else. This finding has been replicated so many times that it has taken on the "status of an empirical generalization" (DeMaris & Rao, 1992, p. 189). Those who cohabit are believed to be more accepting of divorce and less committed to marriage *to begin with* (i.e., regardless of any effect of cohabitation) than those who marry without ever having cohabited. This is described as a "selection" effect. Booth and Johnson (1988) concluded that the most likely explanation for the poorer *marital* quality of those who cohabited prior to marriage is their "deviant lifestyle or a disregard for the traditional norms of society," (p. 270) not something about cohabitation per se. DeMaris and MacDonald (1993), on the other hand, found evidence to suggest that cohabitation appeals to men who are *more conventional* regarding parental obligations and to women who tend to value a *traditional* lifestyle. Whether such differences existed prior to cohabitation or were a result of it could not be determined. Schoen and Weinick (1993) showed that partner-choice criteria differ between cohabiting relationships and marriages, suggesting that "a different kind of relationship calls for a different kind of partner" (p. 413).

There is evidence that the experience of cohabitation fosters values that make divorce more acceptable as a solution to problems. . . . Axinn and Thornton (1992) found that "the same attitudes which increase the rate of cohabitation decrease the rate of marriage" (p. 367)—supporting the "selection" explanation. However, these same authors found that "cohabitation has a causal influence on susceptibility to divorce" (p. 371). In sum, cohabitation has been shown to attract a different type of couple than marriage, and to foster attitudes that contribute to divorce.

Findings such as these suggest that cohabitation and marriage are qualitatively different types of relationships (i.e., cohabitation attracts a different type of person than marriage does, or cohabitation fosters attitudes and beliefs inconsistent with marriage). . . .

. . . This research tests the basic proposition that marriage and cohabitation are qualitatively different forms of relationships as a consequence of sociological processes related to the difference in the two types of unions.

Cohabitation and Marriage: Qualitatively Different Relationships

That people who cohabit are more divorce-prone than those who do not suggests that the nature of cohabiting and married relationships is, in some ways, incompatible. Cohabitation may attract the divorce prone and may produce attitudes and values that lead to divorce. Both possibilities have received empirical support. . . . Knowing this, however, still leaves us unclear about how and why the two types of relationships differ. Drawing from the limited empirical research on this subject, as well as from established sociological theory, the following are offered as dimensions that are predicted to differ qualitatively between cohabitation and marriage. Some dimensions are specific to the relationship whereas others are characteristics of the individual with potential relevance for the relationship.

These dimensions are not presumed to be exhaustive. Rather, each is suggested by prior research or theory on marriage or cohabitation. Broadly, the attempt here is to identify conspicuous features of relationships that are predicted to differ because of the *institutionalization* of the partnership (e.g., legal *vs.* extralegal; normatively approved *vs.* emerging and novel). The following section describes each dimension and provides theoretical justification for its inclusion.

Commitment. The absence of any formally recognized status makes cohabitation quite different from marriage legally. Legal unions are more stable than nonlegal unions. That is, regardless of how a union began (by marriage or cohabitation), the current legal status is a strong predictor of its stability (Teachman, Thomas, & Paasch, 1991). Marriage differs so much from cohabitation legally because of the durability of the commitments involved. Even after a divorce, one may be held legally obligated to an ex-spouse (and to children). There are occasional instances in which courts have awarded limited support to unmarried estranged partners. However, such awards are extremely rare compared to the comparable situation in divorces. Moreover, the legal events of marriage (e.g., formalization of the union requiring significant effort to terminate it or legal assumptions about joint property) serve as what George Levinger (1976) called *barriers* that hold the relationship together. Barriers are things that hold two persons in their relationship in addition to, or even in the absence of, their interpersonal attraction. Property interests embodied in matrimonial law are a significant example of such barriers. Therefore, we expect lower levels of commitment between cohabiting rather than married partners.

Intergenerational relationships. Beyond the absence of formal legal recognition of cohabitation, there is also the absence of clearly defined normative social patterning. Andrew Cherlin (1978) once referred to remarriage as an "incomplete institution" because there were so few socially agreed upon standards governing it. Surely, cohabitation is also an incomplete institution suffused with ambiguity about even such simple issues as what one calls one's cohabiting partner, or the nature of the relationship between a child and the parent's cohabiting partner. American society may lack complete consensus on what it means to be a husband or a wife, but there are clearly traditional standards of propriety and decorum associated with one's relationships with married individuals. Newly married couples quickly realize that they are treated differently once they are married than they were before, especially by parents. By comparison, we lack consensus over what it means to be a cohabiting partner. Cherlin argued that the lack of social norms governing remarriage contributed to high dissolution rates in such relationships. The same may be true of cohabiting relationships. Those in a relationship that is less socially recognized or governed by clear normative standards are less likely to be tightly integrated into networks of others who are in more traditional relationships. This is particularly problematic to the extent that it involves relations between parents and adult children. Cohabitation may, in fact, be a barrier to close relationships across generations.

One of the many forms of possible close social connections, "the parent/(adult) child relationship is a particularly strong and unique source of social integration for parents and adult children" (Umberson, 1992, p. 665). As Umberson notes, the permanence and involuntary origin of the relationship make it particularly significant. Her research revealed significant differences in the extensiveness and nature of such relationships, depending on adult children's marital status. Divorced children (and therefore those in a less socially patterned relationship) received less support from both parents and experienced more strained relationships with others. Never-married children were also found to express strained relationships with their mothers (Umberson, 1992, p. 668). Similar results were found by Cooney and Uhlenberg (1992) in their analysis of the National Survey of Families and Households (NSFH). They found that married children are more likely than unmarried children to cite parents as a source of potential help.

Relationships with parents are potentially important for the overall quality of the husband-wife or cohabiting couple partnership. Those who have poor relationships with their parents lack a basic emotional (and possibly economic) resource. Should the parent-child relationship suffer as a result of a marriage or cohabiting relationship (as a result of parental disapproval of a partner or other aspects of a union) the quality of the partner's affectionate bonds may suffer.

Cohabiting individuals are predicted to report poorer quality intergenerational relationships than married individuals.

Relationship quality. Research already cited has revealed that prior cohabitors have poorer quality marriages than those who did not cohabit prior to marriage. This has been attributed to the probable *selectivity* of cohabitation. That is, those who cohabit eschew tradition and are less committed to a traditional lifestyle. An equally plausible and complementary explanation, however, focuses on the *enforced intimacy* of marriage. There is greater commitment required in marriage. Further, there are stronger social sanctions associated with deviations from tradition in marriage than from cohabitation (e.g., there is stronger social disapproval of "deviant" marital behaviors such as adultery than there is of comparable behavior among unmarried individuals). Together, this means that the relationship between a married couple is harder to dissolve and is supported by stronger social norms than is true for cohabiting individuals. As such, married individuals are more likely to resolve their problems, or at least arrive at acceptable compromises than cohabiting individuals whose relationships are less *enforced* by social and legal constraints. Indeed, one of the arguments offered for the higher divorce rates of prior cohabitors is their belief that escape is a solution to relationship problems (Axinn & Thornton, 1992). Thus the quality of the relationships is predicted to be higher among married than cohabiting individuals.

Ideal fertility. Marriage has traditionally been viewed as the acceptable arrangement for the bearing and rearing of children. Even in the presence of higher rates of out-of-wedlock childbearing, nonmarital fertility is still viewed as less desirable than marital fertility. It has been argued that having a child, or desiring one, is a fundamental difference between cohabiting and married couples (Bachrach, 1987; Rindfuss & VandenHeuvel, 1990). Cohabiting individuals may desire several children, but not with the current partner. Still, in the aggregate we would expect that those who intend to have children will be more likely to marry than those who do not, and those who intend to remain childless will be more likely than those who desire children to enter a cohabiting relationship. Indeed, in light of the traditional association of marriage and childbearing, those who do not intend to have children may have considerably less incentive to marry at all. Research by Rindfuss and VandenHeuvel (1990) found that the percentage of cohabitors intending to have a child in the next 2 years was almost 40% lower than the percentage of married individuals. Indeed, they suggest that on this and other important issues, cohabitors are more similar to single people than married people. Therefore, married individuals are predicted to express higher fertility intentions than cohabiting individuals.

❂ A Note on Racial and Gender Differences

Although there are many racial differences in patterns of marriage and divorce, virtually no research on cohabitation makes racial comparisons. However, in their analysis of the NSFH, Bumpass, Sweet, and Cherlin (1991) showed that cohabitation compensated more for the overall drop in marriage rates among Blacks than among Whites (i.e., increases in cohabitation offset more of the declines in marriage among Blacks than among Whites). Among Blacks, cohabitation compensated for 83% of the overall decline in marriage rates by age 25. Among Whites, it compensated for only 61% (p. 916). Estimates from the NSFH show one quarter (25.4%) of Blacks, 20.2% of Hispanics, and 13.6% of Whites currently cohabiting.

In her analysis of the NSFH, Manning (1993) found that race and age interact to influence the likelihood of legitimating a nonmarital pregnancy. Cohabitation (vs. not cohabiting) is not associated with differential probabilities of marrying to legitimate a pregnancy for teenage girls (regardless of race). However, older pregnant White women who are cohabiting are more likely to marry than comparable women who are not cohabiting (p. 847). Such patterns suggest that research on cohabitation should consider possible moderating influences of race on the distinction between marriage and cohabitation.

Because cohabitation substitutes more for marriage among Blacks than Whites (Bumpass et al., 1991), and because higher rates of cohabitation among Blacks have been interpreted to reflect the fact that cohabitation "has come to be acceptable and almost respectable" in the Black community (Billingsley, 1992, p. 38), smaller cohabitation/marriage differences were predicted among non-Whites than among Whites.

A moderating influence of gender was expected in light of research suggesting that for men, cohabitation is associated with lower levels of commitment to and responsibility for their partner (i.e., unconventional attitudes). The same research found that among women, cohabitation is associated with more conventional family lifestyle attitudes (e.g., disapproval of divorce, individual freedom in marriage, approval of mutual aid among family members). "Although somewhat counterintuitive, this may simply reflect that cohabitation is attractive to women primarily because it is felt to ensure the stability of subsequent marriage" (DeMaris & MacDonald, 1993, p. 404). In light of these findings, smaller cohabitation/marriage differences were expected among females than among males.

☻ Data and Measures

Data for this research were taken from the National Survey of Families and Households (NSFH), a national sample of 13,017 individuals interviewed between March 1987 and May 1988. Cohabiting couples were oversampled to augment the number of such cases. In each selected household, a randomly selected adult was interviewed and (when appropriate) a self-administered questionnaire was completed by the spouse or cohabiting partner. In all, 6,881 married couples and 682 cohabiting couples were included. Of those, spouse questionnaires were completed by 5,684 married spouses and 519 cohabiting partners.

Cohabiting relationships do not endure as long as marriages. For that reason, the analysis is restricted to relationships of no more than 10 years duration. This restriction excludes a large number of marriages, but very few cohabiting relationships. If this is not done, however, a comparison of marriages and cohabitation will be confounded by the fact that the average marriage is much "older" than the average cohabitation. By imposing this restriction, two samples are produced that are closer in terms of duration than would be obtained in a sample of all cohabiting and married couples (average duration of marriages in the analysis sample = 5.4 years; of cohabiting relationships = 2.9 years). The samples may be regarded as representative of individuals in marriage and cohabiting relationships of no more than 10 years duration in the United States. The analysis sample consists of 2,493 married pairs and 499 cohabiting pairs of individuals.

. . .

❂ Results

. . . Selecting only those in relationships of 10 or fewer years minimized the difference between married and cohabiting individuals on the length of their relationships, but there still remains a 2-year difference in average duration. Differences in age, income, and education are consistent with other research on this topic. Cohabitors of both sexes report fewer years of completed schooling and are younger; cohabiting males report lower incomes than married men (see Sweet & Bumpass, 1987). . .

Commitment. The results . . . show several consistent differences between married and cohabiting individuals. Because cohabitation is constrained by fewer social and legal rules than marriage, it was anticipated that the *exit costs* (a measure of commitment) of leaving a cohabiting relationship would be less than those associated with ending a marriage. Cohabiting males and females report that ending their relationship would have move positive (and/or fewer negative) consequences than do either group of married individuals. Commitment, in short, is lower in cohabitation than in marriage.

Intergenerational relationships. Cohabiting individuals report poorer relationships with both mothers and fathers than married individuals. The one exception to this general finding is that males who cohabited with their current spouse do not differ significantly for cohabiting males in their description of the relationships they have with their fathers. Still, bearing this one exception in mind, there is clear and persuasive evidence of poorer intergenerational relations among cohabiting than among married individuals.

Partner relationship quality. The first measure of relationship quality refers to the frequency of disagreements. For both males and females, there does not appear to be any significant difference between married and cohabiting individuals. The second measure of relationship quality is the response to the direct question about overall happiness with the relationship. Relationship happiness is found to differ significantly, depending on whether one is married or cohabiting. Cohabitors report significantly lower levels of happiness than married individuals. This is particularly noteworthy because very few people in relationships describe themselves as *un*happy. . . .

The third measure of relationship quality pertains to fairness in the relationship. There are no differences between married and cohabiting males or females in their perceptions of fairness. . . .

Fertility intentions. For males, ideal fertility is the same for married and cohabiting individuals. However, cohabiting women report lower levels of ideal fertility than their married counterparts who did not cohabit prior to marriage.

To summarize, on issues of commitment, intergenerational relations, and expressed happiness with the relationship, there are broad differences between most married and cohabiting individuals in the direction hypothesized. Consistent differences were not discovered on measures of relationship fairness, frequency of disagreements, and intended fertility.

If we compare responses to questions about the mundane aspects of the present relationship with those having to do with the future or parents, we see a consistent pattern. When asked to speculate about how a separation would affect their lives, cohabiting individuals reported significantly fewer negative consequences than married persons. Similarly, when asked about their relationships with their parents, cohabiting individuals reported them to be of poorer quality than most of their married counterparts (there was but one exception). By way of contrast, issues of relationship fairness (as studied here) pertain to the two partners in their everyday circumstances. The same is true of disagreements. On these measures, there are no differences between married and cohabiting individuals. To the extent that these measures tap the ordinary life of partners, it may be that marriages and cohabiting relationships do not differ very much in their routine and mundane aspects.

The absence of consistent differences in intended fertility is open to several interpretations. One is that fertility intentions are independent of marital status. More likely, however, is that individuals who desire and are presently cohabiting expect to marry (either their current partner or another) before beginning their childbearing. . . .

The distinction between the present partner relationship and concerns about future or more distant issues may be part of a critical underlying difference between marriage and cohabitation. When focused on the immediate issue of daily life, partners in the two types of relationships may be similar. When confronted with concerns about the future, or relations with parents, there may be consistent differences.

Whether these differences are viewed as cause, consequence, or correlate of the type of relationship, the indisputable difference in reported happiness with the relationship is a central finding. Cohabitors report lower levels of happiness with their relationship than married people. Whether overall happiness is a reflection of the current state of affairs, a reflection of long-term concerns, or both, is not really known. Yet if this global assessment is taken to indicate concerns about both, then cohabitors' lower commitments to their relationships and poorer familial relationships are consistent with a poorer assessment of the present relationship.

To investigate this possibility (i.e., reported happiness is a function of the other dimensions considered in the research), a final [analysis was done]. . . . There was at least some evidence of differences associated with marital/cohabiting status. . . . Relationship happiness [is seen] as a consequence of commitment, intergenerational relations, and intended fertility though it could be argued that all such factors are reciprocally linked. Without denying such a possibility, the logic of this research . . . [suggests] marriage *creates* enduring commitments, through law, though it does not create happiness. . . .

The first thing to note is that the simple distinctions between cohabitation and marriage (with or without prior cohabitation) are not significant as they were in the previous analysis, which did not include the measures of commitment, intergenerational relations, and fertility intentions. When the effects of these three factors are considered, significant effects for commitment and intergenerational relations are found, but not for intended fertility. . . . Finally, for men, better relations with their mothers are of much greater importance for relationship happiness than those with their fathers. For women, there is no appreciable difference (i.e., better relations with either parent are associated with comparably better evaluations of the present relationship).

Together, these results suggest that much, if not most, of the difference in relationship quality found to be associated with cohabitation, as opposed to marriage, is actually due to different levels of commitment and differences in the quality of relationships with parents. Cohabitation, that is, appears to take its toll in relationship quality because cohabitors have poorer relations with their parents and have lower levels of commitment—and these foster poorer assessments of the relationship. . . .

◎ Conclusion

This research takes us one step closer toward understanding the nature of the difference between cohabitation and marriage. Married and cohabiting individuals describe their relationships differently. Specifically, cohabitors report lower levels of happiness with their partnerships, express lower degrees of commitment to their relationships, and have poorer quality relationships with their parents. These differences are consistent with the sociological processes hypothesized to produce them: the lack of formal legal or normative structure for cohabitation and the enforced intimacy of marriage. One interpretation of such findings is that cohabitation and marriage do not differ so much in terms of the ordinary, everyday partnerships as they do with respect to long-term concerns and relationships with people beyond the immediate dyad.

The unanswered question raised repeatedly in this and other research is whether cohabitation attracts a different type of person initially or whether the experience itself should be credited with producing observed differences between cohabitation and marriage. In fact, both processes are relevant. Some clues to the relative importance of the two may be found in results comparing those who married after cohabiting with their partner and those who married someone with whom they never had cohabited. In all but one case, when one category of married persons differed from cohabitors, so did the other. Moreover, tests for differences between the two types of *married individuals* . . . supported this general conclusion. Although there were many cases in which the two groups of married individuals differed significantly, the magnitude of those differences were generally less than one half of that found between cohabitors and either married group. The one notable exception is for disagreement frequency. Married individuals differ significantly on this measure, depending on whether they did or did not cohabit with their current spouse before marriage, even when neither group differs significantly from cohabitors. Within the limits of the analysis conducted, those who married after cohabiting appear more similar to those who married without cohabiting than to those who are currently cohabiting. This suggests that the structural and institutional aspects of marriage discussed at the outset of this article define much of the differences between marriage and cohabitation. The results also lend further support to prior research and cohabitation. The results also lend further support to prior research (see Thompson and Colella, 1992) indicating that selection effects are relevant (though perhaps less so than the nature of the relationship) in understanding differences between married and cohabiting individuals.

In considering the differences between marriages and cohabiting relationships, it is important to recognize the durability of commitments embodied in matrimonial law and the enforced intimacy in marriage (i.e., the greater effort required to terminate it). Moreover, although mate-selection is certainly not strongly controlled by parents, mothers and fathers are, nonetheless, conspicuous parties to most marriages. Relations with parents and in-laws in marriage may be difficult at times, but both sets of relatives are recognized to have legitimate interests in their offspring's marriages. In contrast, cohabitation is an incomplete institution. No matter how widespread the practice, nonmarital unions are not yet governed by strong consensual norms or formal laws. What is the legitimate role of a parent in her daughter's cohabiting union? What is the nonmarital equivalent of an in-law? Answers to such questions will emerge if cohabitation persists as a popular form of intimate relationship. For the time being, however, the absence of such institutional norms is a plausible explanation for much of the poorer quality of cohabiting relationships.

References

Axinn, W. G., & Thornton, A. (1992). The relationship between cohabitation and divorce: Selectivity or causal influence? *Demography, 29,* 357–374.

Bachrach, C. A. (1987). Cohabitation and reproductive behavior in the U.S. *Demography, 24,* 623–637.

Billingsley, A. (1992). *Climbing Jacob's ladder.* New York: Simon and Schuster.

Booth, A., & Johnson, D. (1988). Premarital cohabitation and marital success. *Journal of Family Issues, 9,* 255–272.

Booth, A., & White, L. (1980). Thinking about divorce. *Journal of Marriage and the Family, 42,* 605–36.

Bumpass, L. L., & Sweet, J. A. (1989). National estimates of cohabitation. *Demography, 26,* 615–625.

Bumpass, L. L., Sweet, J. A., & Cherlin, A. J. (1991). The role of cohabitation in declining rates of marriage. *Journal of Marriage and the Family, 53,* 913–927.

Cherlin, A. J. (1978). Remarriage as an incomplete institution. *American Journal of Sociology, 84,* 634–50.

Cherlin, A. J. (1992). *Marriage, divorce, and remarriage* (Rev. ed.). Cambridge, MA: Harvard University Press.

Cooney, T. M., & Uhlenberg, P. (1992). Support from parents over the life course: The adult child's perspective. *Social Forces, 71,* 63–84.

DeMaris, A., & MacDonald, W. (1993). Premarital cohabitation and marital instability: A test of the unconventionality hypothesis. *Journal of Marriage and the Family, 55,* 399–407.

DeMaris, A., & Rao, V. (1992). Premarital cohabitation and subsequent marital stability in the United States: A reassessment. *Journal of Marriage and the Family, 54,* 178–190.

Glenn, N. D., & McLanahan, S. (1982). Children and marital happiness: A further specification of the relationship. *Journal of Marriage and the Family, 44,* 63–72.

Johnson, D. R., White, L. K., Edwards, J. N., & Booth, A. (1986). Dimensions of marital quality. *Journal of Family Issues, 7,* 31–49.

Langman, L. (1987). Social stratification. In M. B. Sussman & S. K. Steinmetz (Eds.), *Handbook of marriage and the family* (pp. 211–249). New York: Plenum.

Levinger, G. (1976). A social psychological perspective on marital dissolution. *Journal of Social Issues, 35,* 50–78.

Manning, W. D. (1993). Marriage and cohabitation following premarital conception. *Journal of Marriage and the Family, 55,* 839–850.

Nock, S. L., (1979). The family life cycle: Empirical or conceptual tool? *Journal of Marriage and the Family, 40,* 15–26.

Rank, M. R. (1982). Determinants of conjugal influence in wives' employment decision making. *Journal of Marriage and the Family, 44,* 591–604.

Rindfuss, R. R., & VandenHeuvel, A. (1990). Cohabitation: A precursor to marriage or an alternative to being single? *Population and Development Review, 40,* 703–726.

Rossi, A. S., & Rossi, P. H. (1990). *Of human bonding.* New York: Aldine de Gruyter.

Schoen, R., & Weinick, R. M. (1993). Partner choice in marriages and cohabitation. *Journal of Marriage and the Family, 54,* 408–414.

Schumm, W. R., & Bugaighis, M. A. (1986). Marital quality over the marital career: Alternative explanations. *Journal of Marriage and the Family, 48,* 165–168.

Suitor, J. J. (1991). Marital quality and satisfaction with the division of household labor across the life cycle. *Journal of Marriage and the Family, 53,* 221–30.

Sweet, J. A., & Bumpass, L. L. (1987). *American families and households.* New York: Russell Sage.

Teachman, J. D., Thomas, J. J., & Paasch, K. (1991). Legal status and the stability of coresidential unions. *Demography, 28,* 571–586.

Teachman, J. D., Polonko, K. A., & Scanzoni, J. J. (1987). Demography of the family. In M. B. Sussman & S. K. Steinmetz (Eds.), *Handbook of marriage and the family* (pp. 3–36). New York: Plenum.

Thompson, E., & Colella, U. (1992). Cohabitation and marital stability: Quality or commitment? *Journal of Marriage and the Family, 54,* 259–267.

Umberson, D. (1992). Relations between adult children and parents: Psychological consequences for both generations. *Journal of Marriage and the Family, 54,* 664–674.

U.S. Bureau of the Census. (1989). *Marital status and living arrangements: 1989* (Series P-20, No. 433). Washington, DC: U.S. Government Printing Office.

U.S. Bureau of the Census. (1992). *Marital status and living arrangements: 1992* (Series P-20 No. 468). Washington, DC: U.S. Government Printing Office.

Yogev, S., & Brett, J. (1985). Perceptions of the division of housework and child care and marital satisfaction. *Journal of Marriage and the Family, 47,* 609–618.

❧ ❧ ❧

Questions

1. Why are those who cohabit more prone to divorce than those who marry?

2. Why has remarriage been called an "incomplete institution"? Would you argue that cohabitation is also an incomplete institution? Explain your answer.

3. In what ways can the relationships of those who cohabit be seen as less successful than the relationships of those who are married? In what ways might they be more successful?

4. What differences did Nock find between the relationships of cohabiting couples and those of married couples?

5. Do you think that Americans will ever value cohabitation in the same way that they do marriage? Why or why not?

Making Ends Meet on a Welfare Check

KATHRYN EDIN AND LAURA LEIN

This selection is a compelling look at how welfare mothers sustain their families on various cash and non-cash assistance. Kathryn Edin and Laura Lein portray what living on welfare is like. Having conducted research through in-depth interviews, they detail how much money "welfare mothers" spend each month on basic necessities. They then contrast the families' expenses with the amount of support they receive through various funding mechanisms including welfare, food stamps, Section 8 housing assistance, and Aid to Families with Dependent Children (AFDC). Edin and Lein observe the discrepancy between the families' necessary expenses and their income and ask the logical question, How do welfare mothers "make the ends meet?"

Along Minnesota's Highway 72—which runs between the Canadian border town of Rainy River and Bemidji, Minnesota—a large, crudely lettered billboard greets the southbound traveler:

WELCOME TO MINNESOTA

LAND OF 10,000 TAXES

BUT WELFARE PAYS GOOD

Antiwelfare sentiment is common among Minnesotans, who live in a state with high personal income taxes and cash welfare benefits substantially above the national median. But even in southern states, where cash welfare benefits are very low and taxes modest, citizens are likely to denigrate welfare. In 1990, about 40 percent of respondents in each region told interviewers from the National Opinion Research Center that the United States spends too much on welfare.[1] In 1994, another nationally representative survey found that 65 percent of Americans believed welfare spending was too high (Blendon et al. 1995).

Legislators recognize welfare's unpopularity. In the first half of the

1990s, several states cut benefits, and all let their value lag behind inflation. In addition, most states applied for federal waivers to experiment with benefit limitations or sanctions not allowed by the old federal rules. Some states established a "family cap," which, denied additional cash to mothers who had another child while receiving welfare. In other states, mothers whose children were truant from school lost a portion of their cash grant. Furthermore, under the new federal rules, all states must limit the amount of time a mother spends on welfare to five years.

Public dissatisfaction with welfare persists despite the fact that cash benefits to welfare recipients have declined by more than 40 percent in real terms since the mid-1970s (Blank 1994, 179). The reasons for the continuing public discontent throughout this period are complex, but probably rest on the widespread belief that the federal welfare entitlement perpetuated laziness and promiscuity (Bobo and Smith 1994; Page and Shapiro 1992).[2] Lazy women had babies to get money from the welfare system, the story went, and then let lazy boyfriends share their beds and live off their benefits. These lazy and immoral adults then raised lazy and immoral children, creating a vicious cycle of dependency.

Those who have promoted this view include the news media and talk show hosts, but social scientists also have contributed. The most widely known "scientific" argument was developed by Charles Murray, who in 1984 claimed that welfare actually makes the poor worse off. Federal welfare became too generous during the 1960s and 1970s, Murray argued, and began to reward unwed motherhood and indolence over marriage and jobs (Murray 1984). Social scientists spent much of the late 1980s attempting to discover whether Murray was right. Typically, economists judged the merits of the claim by estimating the disincentive effects of more or less generous state welfare benefits on work (for a review of this literature, see Moffitt 1992). Other researchers attempted to measure the effect of varying state benefits on marriage, divorce, and remarriage (Bane and Ellwood 1994).

The task we set for ourselves in this chapter is a more fundamental one. In order to assess whether any welfare program is too generous, one must compare its benefits to the cost of living faced by that program's recipients. An obvious starting point is to ask how much families headed by single mothers spend each month to make ends meet, and how that income compares with what they receive from welfare.

◉ How Much do Welfare-Reliant Mothers Spend?

In 1992, Donna Carson, a forty-year-old African American mother of two living in San Antonio, characterized herself as "ambitious and determined." She had spent most of her adult life playing by the rules. After high school graduation, she got a job and got married. She conceived her first child at age twenty-five, but her husband left before the child was born. Soon after her son's birth, she arranged for her mother to take care of him and went back to work. Because she did not have to pay for child care, her wages from her nurse's aide job combined with the child support she received from her ex-husband were enough to pay the bills. Ten years later, when she turned thirty-six, she had a second child. This time she was not married to the father. Carson's mother was willing to watch this child as well, so again she returned to work. Shortly thereafter, Carson's father's diabetes worsened and both of his legs were amputated. Her mother was overwhelmed by the tragedy and checked herself into a psychiatric hospital, leaving Carson to care for her two children and her disabled father alone. Seeing no other way out, she quit her job and turned to welfare. That was 1989.

Three years later, when we were talking with her, Carson was still on welfare, and her budget was tight. Her typical monthly expenditures were about $920 a month. One-third of that amount went to rent and utilities, another third went to food, and the rest went to cover her children's clothing, their school supplies, her transportation, and all the other things the family needed. Her combined monthly benefits from AFDC and food stamps, however, came to only $477.

Some months, she received a "pass through" child support payment of $50 from the father of her first child, who was legally obligated to pay. Although this payment did not reduce her AFDC benefits, her food stamps did go down by about $15 every time she received it. The father of her second child bypassed the formal child support system and paid her $60 directly each month. To get the rest of the money she needed, Carson took care of a working neighbor's child during the day. This neighbor could pay only $100 a month, but gave her the money in cash so that Carson's welfare caseworker could not detect the earnings and reduce her check. She got the rest of the money she needed from her father, who paid her $250 in cash each month to care for him.

TABLE 1 *Monthly Expenses of 214 AFDC Recipients: Means and Standard Deviations*

	Mean	SID
Housing costs	$213	$187
Food costs	262	112
Other necessities	336	176
Medical	18	43
Clothing	69	62
Transportation	62	83
Child care	7	32
Phone	31	35
Laundry/toiletries/cleaning supplies	52	31
Baby care	18	32
School supplies and fees	14	48
Appliance and furniture	17	39
Miscellaneous	47	59
Nonessentials	64	63
Entertainment	20	31
Cable TV	6	14
Cigarettes and alcohol	22	30
Eat out	13	27
Lottery costs	3	16
TOTAL EXPENSES	876	283

Source: Authors' calculations using Edin and Lein survival strategies data.
Note: The mean family size is 3.17 people. Numbers do not total due to rounding.

Though Carson had more personal tragedy than most, her budget was similar to that of most other welfare recipients we talked with. Table 1 gives the monthly expenses of the 214 welfare-reliant mothers we interviewed (and their 464 children). It shows that our respondents averaged $213 a month on housing, $262 on food, $336 on other necessary expenses, and $64 on items that were arguably not essential—a total of $876 for an average family of 3.17 people.[3]

Housing Expenses

The housing expenses of welfare-reliant families varied substantially. This variation depended on whether recipients paid market rent, had a housing subsidy in a public housing project or a private building (Section 8), or shared housing with a relative or friend. Donna Carson paid market rent, which in San Antonio was quite low but still higher than what most mothers pay in subsidized units. However, apartments that meet the physical criteria required for Section 8 tended to be in neighborhoods with less access to public transportation than the neighborhoods where housing projects were generally located, so these families usually had to maintain an automobile. Consequently, while public housing and Section 8 residents paid roughly the same amount for housing, Section 8 families spent far more for transportation.

In most cases, the welfare-reliant families who shared housing with a friend or relative were able to split the rent, utilities, telephone bill, and other household expenses. Thus, their expenses for rent and these other items were relatively low. About half of those who shared housing lived with one or both parents. The other half lived with siblings or friends. Mothers who lived with a parent usually made only token contributions toward the rent and took some portion of the responsibility for utilities and household maintenance. Most lived with their parents precisely because they could not afford to maintain their own households. Those who lived with a sibling or friend usually paid half of the household expenses. Sometimes, however, mothers "rented" only a portion of the living space (a single room, for example) and paid only a quarter or a third of the household costs.[4]

Food Expenses

Food expenditures averaged $262 a month for the welfare-reliant families we interviewed. This means that these mothers spent $19 per person on food in a typical week. This amount is nearly identical to the federal government's cheap food plan (the "thrifty food budget"), which uses as its base what poor mothers bought for their families in the 1950s and adjusts the prices in that "basket" for inflation each year (Ruggles 1990; Schwarz and Volgy 1992). The average weekly food stamp allotment for the families we interviewed, however, was slightly lower than this amount—$16 per person. This is because we oversampled mothers with housing subsidies to try to find mothers who could live on their benefits alone, and they do not qualify for the maximum amount of food stamps (food stamps are adjusted for living costs). This meant that the average mother had to cover $40 of food expenses each month with income from some source other than food stamps.[5]

Food stamp benefits also varied with family income, including cash welfare. In the lowest AFDC benefit states, therefore, families could receive up to $292 a month in food stamps for a family of three, or $21 per person per week in 1991, and families in these sites who reported no outside income received this maximum. Most found it sufficient to cover the bulk of their food expenditures. Families in states that paid more generous welfare benefits received roughly 30 cents less in food stamps for each additional dollar in cash welfare benefits. Because of this, hardly anyone who lived outside the South could pay their food bills with food stamps alone.[6] In San Antonio, food stamps covered 99 percent of respondents' average food expenditures; in Charleston, 88 percent; in Chicago, 80 percent; and in high-benefit Boston, only 65 percent.

Other Expenses

Besides housing and food, clothing took the next biggest bite out of the average family's monthly budget, followed by transportation, laundry and toiletries, telephone charges, medical expenses, baby care, and appliance and furniture costs. On average, welfare reliant mothers spent $69 a month on clothing. This means that the mothers with whom we spoke typically purchased $261 worth of shoes, coats, and other apparel for each family member in a year.[7] Most of this was for their children, since children continually grow out of their clothing.

Welfare-reliant mothers employed a number of strategies to contain their clothing expenditures. Virtually all purchased some of their clothing at thrift or second-hand stores, and most scoured neighborhood yard sales. During our interviews, many mothers proudly showed us their second-hand buys: a barely worn pair of name-brand jeans or a winter coat that was practically new and only a bit too small. A mother's largest expense in the clothing category was for children's shoes. Children not only went through two or more pairs of shoes a year, but shoes in children's sizes and in good condition were seldom available at neighborhood thrift stores. Winter coats, hats, mittens, and boots were also expensive, and most children grew out of them every other winter. Thus in the winter months, clothing needs could become an added hardship. One mother told us,

> In the winter months, I have had to keep my children at home on the really cold days because I didn't have warm enough clothes to dress them. I have learned to swallow my pride, though, and go to the second-hand shops and try to get the right kind of winter clothes for the boys.

The welfare-reliant mothers we interviewed felt that second-hand clothing was acceptable for younger children, whose peers were still largely unconcerned with appearance. One mother told us,

> For shopping I go to yard sales and the Salvation Army for Jay's clothes. Fortunately, he isn't the type of kid who always has to have Nike sneakers or he won't go to school. I get him K-Mart ones, or I go to the used clothes store [on] Belmont [Avenue]. I probably spend $200 a season on new clothes for him, but some of those he can wear from season to season.

Other mothers reported that their older children—especially high school boys—felt they could not maintain their self-respect or the respect of their peers while wearing K-Mart shoes to school. Some mothers felt that if they did not purchase name-brand sneakers, an athletic jacket, or other popular items for their teenagers, their children might be lured into criminal activity so they could buy these items themselves:

> My boy, he sees these kids that sell drugs. They can afford to buy these [tennis shoes] and he can't. So I have my little side-job and [I buy them for him]. You got to do it to keep them away from drugs, from the streets.

One mother told us that in order to buy her child a $50 pair of tennis shoes, she ate only one meal a day for a month. The savings in her food bill were enough to cover the purchase of the shoes. Most mothers in her neighborhood did not feel it was necessary to go hungry to meet their children's clothing needs, because they could generate the extra cash in other ways, which we discuss later.

Mothers who bought new clothing generally had to put the clothing on layaway. They paid a small portion of the purchase price each month. Some others found professional shoplifters who would note the children's sizes, shoplift the clothing, and sell it for a fraction of the ticket price to the mother.

Transportation cost the average welfare-reliant family $62 a month. Families living in Charleston (where there was little access to public transportation) and families living outside central cities spent more because they had to maintain automobiles or pay for taxis. At the time of our interviews, welfare rules limited the value of a family's automobile to $2,500. This meant that mothers had older cars, which generally required more frequent repair and got poorer gas mileage. All of the states we studied had mandatory insurance laws, and respondents told us that minimum insurance coverage cost at least $40 a month. In addition, Chicago and metropolitan Boston required that families purchase city stickers to park on the street, and South Carolina taxed the value of a family's car each year.

Although mothers who had access to public transportation spent less than those mothers who maintained cars, bus and subway transportation cost the average mother who used it more than $60 a month. Few mothers lived in areas where they could walk to the laundromat or the grocery store. In neighborhoods that provided these amenities, rents were higher. Since few mothers could afford child care, a shopping trip required that mothers bring their children with them and pay the bus or subway fares for the older children as well (younger children often ride free).

Laundry, toiletries, and cleaning supplies also constituted a significant proportion of monthly expenses. Some mothers washed their clothing in the bathtub and let it air-dry in their apartment or outside. This was a time-consuming task, however, and mothers complained that their clothes did not get as clean as machine-washed clothing. A few mothers owned or rented their own washers and dryers, but most used local laundromats. Because most families' clothing stock was slim (for example, two or three pairs of pants for each person was typical), mothers usually washed their clothing once each week or more. Laundromat prices varied, but mothers seldom spent less than $6 for coin machines each time they visited the laundromat, for roughly three loads.

All told, the welfare-reliant mothers had to spend $23 in a typical month to wash and dry their clothing and an additional $29 on toiletries and cleaning supplies. Food stamps could not be used to purchase toiletries or cleaning supplies, so mothers had to pay for sponges, cleaning fluids, dishwashing liquid, hand and laundry soap, bleach, toilet paper, hair care products, deodorant, disposable razors, and feminine products with cash.

Ninety-two percent of our sample had telephone service for at least part of the year. On average, families spent $31 monthly on telephone charges. Twenty-six percent of the welfare recipients had their phone disconnected at least once during the past year because of nonpayment. When mothers ran short of money, they were usually more willing to do without a phone than to neglect rent, utilities, food, clothing, transportation, or other essentials. Basic service charges also varied widely by site. in San Antonio, where basic local service cost about $12 a month, families spent only $18 a month for phone-related costs. In all other sites, comparable service ranged from $20 to $25 a month, and families spent much more. These costs included not only charges for local and long-distance calls but connection and reconnection charges as well. Although not strictly necessary for a family's material well-being, mothers without telephones had a difficult time maintaining contact with welfare caseworkers and their children's schools. It was also more difficult to apply for jobs because prospective employers could not reach them to set up an interview. Some solved this dilemma by sharing a phone with a neighbor; messages left with neighbors, however, were not always promptly forwarded.

Medicaid, the government's health insurance program for low-income families, offered free emergency care and routine physician care. All the households in our welfare-reliant sample were covered by Medicaid. Over-the-counter medicines and other medical services, however, were not covered and constituted another $18 of the average welfare-reliant mother's monthly budget. These expenses included routine drugstore costs, such as those for pain relievers, cough syrup, adhesive bandages, vitamin tablets, or other medicines families frequently used. In addition, few state Medicaid programs pay for prescription birth control pills, abortions, antidepressants, or other mental health drugs. Nor do most Medicaid plans pay for dental care, except for emergency oral surgery.

Diapers and other baby care products cost an average welfare-reliant family $18 a month (37 percent of the welfare recipients in our sample had babies in diapers). Welfare-reliant mothers with infants and young toddlers typically received formula, milk, eggs, and cheese from WIC (Women's, Infants', and Children's nutritional program). Most mothers told us, however, that they were usually one or two cans short of formula each month and had to purchase them at the grocery store. In addition, WIC does not provide disposable diapers, which constituted roughly 80 percent of the cash welfare-reliant mothers had to spend on baby care. Only a tiny minority of the mothers we interviewed used cloth diapers; although cheaper than disposables, cloth diapering was not practicable for mothers who relied on laundromats. In addition, mothers who used cloth diapers reported substantial upfront costs (they had to buy the diapers), and these mothers spent substantially more for laundry supplies than other mothers. Mothers also averaged $14 a month on school-related expenses and $7 a month on child care.

Appliances and furniture cost the typical family another $17 a month. Generally mothers purchased both new and used furniture and appliances with installment payments. Because they could not get bank credit, these mothers would often arrange credit at local thrift shops and "rent-to-own" furniture stores. Although local thrift stores did not generally apply finance charges to mothers' purchases (they usually held the item until it was fully paid for), rent-to-own furniture stores did. Because the latter stores charged very high interest rates and allowed long repayment periods, mothers some-times ended up paying two to three times the actual value of the item. Meanwhile, mothers who missed a payment could have the furniture repos-sessed, losing whatever equity they had built up.

Miscellaneous items in the families' budgets included check-cashing fees and fees for money orders, debt service, burial insurance (discussed later in this chapter), and haircuts. These items totaled $47 in the average month.

Nonessentials

Entertainment cost the typical family $20 each month and was usually lim-ited to video rentals; occasionally it included movies, trips to amusement parks, and travel (mothers sometimes sent their children to relatives during the summer). Mothers spent an average of $22 for cigarettes and alcohol each month, mostly on cigarettes. Mothers seldom bought their own alcohol, and those who drank depended on boyfriends, friends, and family members to pay for their drinks. This was also true for most mothers who used marijuana or other drugs. In addition, mothers spent an average of $3 a month for the lottery, $6 a month for cable television, and $13 a month to eat out. All told, the typical welfare-reliant family spent $64 a month on these nonnecessary items, or about 7 percent of their total budget.[8] Although not physical neces-sities, the items met crucial psychological needs.

Although the mothers in our sample worried about day-to-day material survival, most saw survival as having broader "psychological" and "social" dimensions. One mother commented:

> You know, we live in such a materialistic world. Our welfare babies have needs and wants too. They see other kids going to the circus, having toys and stuff like that. You gotta do what you gotta do to make your kid feel normal. There is no way you can deprive your child.

This woman's statement captures a common sentiment among the welfare recipients we interviewed: children need to have an occasional treat, and mothers who refuse them may deprive their offspring of normalcy. Even among Mexican American mothers in San Antonio, who spent less than any of the other welfare-reliant mothers, one family in six paid a small monthly fee for a basic cable subscription. These mothers told us they saw the cable subscription as a cheap way of keeping their kids off the streets and out of trouble.

The mothers themselves needed an occasional boost too. Many reported that by spending small amounts on soda pop, cosmetics, cigarettes, alcohol, or the lottery, they avoided feeling like they were "completely on the bottom," or that their lives were "completely hopeless." When we asked respondents if they could do without them, they replied that these items gave them some measure of self-respect, and without them they would lose hope of bettering their situations:

> I never buy for myself, only for my son. Well, I take that back. I allow myself two of what I guess you would call luxuries. Well, I guess three. First, I buy soda pop. I do not eat meals hardly ever, but I always have to have a can of Pepsi in my hand. I drink Pepsi nonstop. My boyfriend, he buys it for me by the case 'cause he knows how much I like it, and I guess it's the pop that gives me my energy for dealing with my son—you know, the sugar and caffeine and stuff.

> And then I treat myself to the cigarettes. Without the smoking, I would just worry all the time about how we was going to eat and would never relax. I feel like I deserve some little pleasure, you know, and so those cigarettes keep me up, keep me feeling that things aren't so bad.

> And the other thing is, I buy my cosmetics. I mean, I go around feeling so low all the time, and the makeup makes me feel, you know, better about myself. I feel like I'm not so poor when I can buy myself some cosmetics at the discount house.

The few respondents who spent money on alcohol reported similar sentiments:

> Oh, sometimes, you know, just to relax or somethin', I just go out and have a few. And when I'm really low, I sometimes go out and tie one on, if you know what I mean. Sometimes I think I'll go crazy all day in the house if I can't get out once in a while. I just couldn't take it.

Although few mothers played the lottery with any regularity, those who did also viewed it as a sort of escape:

> I just can't afford not to buy some tickets when the pot gets real big. I sometimes buy five tickets if I can afford it. I like to plan what I'm going to do with it, you know, fantasize and stuff—dream of what it would be like to own nice things and such.

· · ·

⚬ How do Welfare-Reliant Mothers Make Ends Meet?

No one without substantial assets can spend more than they take in for long. The welfare-reliant women we interviewed had few savings, no IRA accounts, no stocks or bonds, and no valuable assets. If they had and if their caseworkers had known, they would have been ineligible for welfare. When they ran out of cash and food stamps, those who did not have a generous parent or boyfriend worked at regular or informal jobs. They also had to "work" the system, making sure that neither their earnings nor the contributions they received came to the attention of the welfare department. If they reported such income, their welfare checks would soon be reduced by almost the full amount of this income, leaving them as poor as before.

Table 2 shows that, on average, cash welfare, food stamps, and SSI covered only about three-fifths of welfare-reliant mothers' expenses.[9] A small amount also came from the earned income tax credit (EITC) for wages earned in the prior year. From our conversations with mothers, we learned that they made up the remaining gap by generating extra cash, garnering in-kind contributions, and purchasing stolen goods at below market value. We found it difficult to estimate, however, how much each mother saved by using the latter two techniques. Therefore, we only present figures for those strategies that generated extra cash.

Earnings from reported work, unreported work (off the books or under a false identity), or work in the underground economy (selling sex, drugs, or stolen goods) made up 15 percent of welfare-reliant mothers' total income.[10] Another chunk (17 percent) came from members of their personal networks and went unreported. Agency-based contributions—usually cash contributions, direct payment of mothers' bills, or the portion of student grants and loans that could be squeezed for extra household cash after paying for tuition and books—covered the last 4 percent of the average welfare-reliant mother's budget.

To get a clearer sense how welfare-reliant mothers generated extra income, Table 2 also shows the degree to which mothers relied on various sources of income each month. By definition, all the mothers we coded as welfare-reliant received something from the AFDC program. Table 2 shows that almost all of them also received food stamps (95 percent), compared with 87 percent of welfare recipients nationwide (U.S. House of Representatives 1993, 711).[11] Nine percent of the sample received SSI or payments for the care of foster children. Seven percent received money from the EITC because they reported income from work during the previous calendar year.

Table 2 gives further detail on how mothers' earnings from work contributed to their family budgets. Five percent worked in the formal economy at reported jobs, compared with 6 percent nationally (U.S. House of

TABLE 2 *Survival Strategies of 214 Welfare-Reliant Mothers*

Variable	Amount of Income Generated Through Each Survival Strategy	Percentage of Total Budget	Percent of Mothers Engaging in Each Survival Strategy[a]
TOTAL EXPENSES	$876	100%	N/A
Housing costs	213	24	N/A
Food costs	262	30	N/A
Other necessities	336	39	N/A
Nonessentials	64	7	N/A
Welfare benefits	565	64	N/A
AFDC	307	35	100%
Food stamps	222	25	95
SSI	36	4	9
EITC	3	2	7
Work-based strategies	128	15	46
Reported work	19	2	5
Unreported work	90	10	39
Underground work	19	2	8
Network-based strategies	151	17	77
Family and friends	62	7	46
Men	95	11	52
Boyfriends	56	6	29
Absent fathers	39	4	33
Covert system	33	4	23
Formal system	7	1	14
Agency-based strategies	37	4	31
TOTAL INCOME	883	100%	N/A

Source: Authors' calculations using Edin and Lein survival strategies data.

Note: These income-generating strategies do not include in-kind contributions or purchasing goods illegally because these figures were difficult to estimate. Columns do not total due to rounding.

[a]The sum of the percentages exceeds the total because some mothers engaged in more than one strategy.

Representatives 1993, 696). Others were also working and not reporting it. Approximately two-fifths (39 percent) worked off the books or under a false identity to generate additional income, and 8 percent worked in the underground economy selling sex, drugs, or stolen goods. (The percentages do not sum to 46 percent because some mothers engaged in more than one strategy.) Table 2 also shows that 77 percent of mothers were currently receiving covert contributions from family, boyfriends, or absent fathers in order to make ends meet.[12] Nearly half (46 percent) of welfare-reliant mothers relied on family and friends for financial help each month. Even more, 52 percent, received help from a man: 29 percent from boyfriends on a regular basis, 14 percent through the formal child support collection system, and 23 percent from the fathers of their children on a covert basis. In addition, 31 percent received cash, voucher, or direct assistance in paying a bill from a community group, charity, or student aid program.

. . .

● Surviving on Welfare

Americans have long worried that welfare benefits are too generous. Many hear about high rates of out-of-wedlock births among the poor and conclude that welfare contributes to the problem. A more fundamental question is how individual welfare recipients actually use the government support they receive? What standard of living do welfare benefits afford single mothers?

We have attempted to answer this question by interviewing 214 welfare-reliant mothers about what they spent to keep their families together. We also examined the level of welfare benefits available to the mothers. We found that for most welfare-reliant mothers food and shelter alone cost almost as much as these mothers received from the government. For more than one-third, food and housing costs exceeded their cash benefits, leaving no extra money for uncovered medical care, clothing, and other household expenses. When we added the costs of other necessities to the mothers' budgets, it was evident that virtually all welfare-reliant mothers experienced a wide gap between what they could get from welfare and what they needed to support their families. In fact, with only one exception, we met no welfare mother who was making ends meet on her government check alone. Mothers filled the gap through reported and unreported work and through handouts from family, friends, and agencies. Finally, we asked the difficult question of whether welfare-reliant mothers' expenditures were truly necessary. We found that our mothers' budgets were far below the household budgets collected by the Consumer Expenditure Survey in 1991 for single-parent families. Our welfare-reliant mothers also spent less than the lowest income group the CES interviewed. Our conclusion is that the vast majority of our welfare-reliant mothers' expenses were at the very low end of widely shared national consumption norms.

Despite spending far more than their welfare benefits, many of the families we interviewed experienced serious material hardship. Variations in benefit levels had real consequences for welfare-reliant single mothers and their children. Lower benefits substantially increased material hardship as did having larger families. Life on welfare, it seems, was an exceedingly tenuous affair.[13] An articulate Chicago respondent put it this way:

> I don't understand why [Public Aid is] punishing people who are poor if you want to mainstream them. If indeed, the idea is to segregate, to be biased, to create a widening gap between the haves and the have-nots, then the welfare system is working. If it is to provide basic needs, not just the financial but psychological and social needs of every human being, then the system fails miserably.

Endnotes

[1]In 1994, 49 percent of Americans thought that welfare programs discouraged people from working, and two-thirds believed that welfare encouraged women to have more children than they would have had if welfare were not available (Blendon and others 1995).

[2]These responses were gathered during the center's General Social Survey.

[3]Due to rounding, these estimates do not total $876.

[4]We did not include any teenage mothers living at home. Mothers under age eighteen constitute only a tiny portion of all mothers on the welfare rolls (U.S. House of Representatives 1995, table 10-27). We did interview seventeen teenage mothers and found that they paid almost none of their own bills because most of them lived rent-free with their mothers while they tried to finish school. Therefore, these teenage mothers could not construct a household budget.

[5]Nor could families with housing subsidies, disability income, or reported outside income buy all of their food with food stamps.

[6]There is a reduction in food stamp benefits as cash benefits rise.

[7]$(69/3.17)*12$

[8]In terms of nonnecessary spending, more than a third of families spent nothing whatsoever on entertainment during the previous year, two-thirds never ate out;

nearly half had spent nothing on cigarettes or alcohol during the year; and four-fifths had gone without cable television.

[9]Four percent of all welfare-reliant families received either SSI or survivor's benefits (U.S. House of Representatives 1993, 719).

[10]For those mothers who sold illegal drugs, a small personal supply was sometimes an in-kind benefit of the job.

[11]These small differences are due to the fact that we did not interview any teenage recipients, who often lived with better-off family members and were thus not eligible for food stamps.

[12]Fourteen percent had received payments through the Child Support Enforcement system in the last year, which was slightly above the national average of 12 percent for welfare recipients (U.S. Department of Health and Human Services 1990, 43).

[13]Whereas Charles Murray portrayed an overly generous welfare system that kept the poor in poverty because it rewarded their indolence, mothers saw welfare as a stingy and punishing system that placed them and their children in a desperate economic predicament.

● ● ●

Questions

1. Why do Americans generally resent welfare assistance programs and welfare recipients?

2. How large is the discrepancy between the funds needed for self-sufficiency and the level of assistance welfare families receive?

3. Do you see any places where welfare mothers could cut their monthly budgets to survive on welfare assistance? Would eliminating certain items be sufficient to get their expenses under budget?

4. Most college students live on what they perceive to be a "bare bones" budget. Find out how much welfare assistance you would qualify for in your residential state. How far above or below this threshold are your current expenses? What in your own monthly budget would you need to eliminate to survive on welfare assistance?

5. What do you speculate are the causes for people living on welfare assistance? Think of causes that include cultural, structural, and normative factors.

If the French Can Do It, Why Can't We?

STEVEN GREENHOUSE

Finding quality, affordable daycare is a problem for many working parents. Some people just don't have the money to pay for good daycare, while others live in communities where demand for care far exceeds the slots available. In this article, Steven Greenhouse describes the French child-care system, which is open to all infants regardless of their parents' ability to pay.

Pascal Favre-Rochex is in the midst of that morning tightrope walk parents know so well—settling his son in preschool. His knees are scrunched up against the pint-size table as he hams it up, reading "Monsieur Rigolo" to 3-year-old Clément. A moment later he gives his son a hug and is out the door. The teacher, Maryse Corne, invites Clément, Antoine, Inès, Mehdi, Stanislas and 16 other toddlers to sit on the gray rug at her feet. First they recite rhymes about escargots and bumblebees and then they sing "Frère Jacques," pumping their right arms up and down to ring imaginary church bells.

By French standards it's just another day in preschool. But through American eyes what's going on in this Parisian preschool is extraordinary. This class is part of a free, full-day, public preschool, or école maternelle. Many New Yorkers, Washingtonians and Californians pay $8,000 to $14,000 a year to send a child to preschool or a day-care center, if they are lucky enough to find a place. In France, 99 percent of 3-, 4- and 5-year-olds attend preschool at no or minimal charge.

In sharp contrast, just one-third of American 3- and 4-year-olds attend preschools or day-care centers, and in many communities, the nonaffluent need not apply. But with the strong backing of left and right, the French spend $7 billion a year to make sure every child—rich, middle class or poor—gets off to a good start. They feel the benefits outweigh the cost.

Comparing the French system with the American system—if that word can be used to describe a jigsaw puzzle missing half its pieces—is like comparing a vintage bottle of Château Margaux with a $4 bottle of American wine. The first child-care centers were built in the early 1800's to protect the children of women who took jobs in rapidly industrializing Paris. But it was only after World War II that the system exploded in size as the battle-scarred nation sought to protect its young from starvation and disease. Today, for France's 4.5 million children under the age of 6, the constellation of child-care offerings is vast and all of them are linked to health care. The three major categories are day-care centers and day-care homes, for children 3 months to 3 years of age, and preschools, for children 2 1/2 to 5 years old. Day-care centers, or crèches and day-care homes charge fees on a sliding scale. Public preschools, or écoles maternelles, are free; parochial preschools are heavily subsidized.

"Our objective is to be both a place of learning and a place that stimulates children," says Josiane Mattei, the director of the preschool Clément attends, off Avenue du Général Leclerc. Mattei coordinates the curriculum for 210 children and, since this is France, sees to it that the children use proper table manners.

"We don't want parents to feel that they're leaving their kids at a baggage claim," she says.

Preschools run from 8:30 A.M. to 4:30 P.M.; parents can pay $300 a year for wraparound programs that provide supervised activities from 7:30 to 8:30 A.M. and 4:30 to 6 P.M.

Local government supports the day-care centers, which are normally open from 7 A.M. to 7 P.M. The overall cost of sending a child to a Parisian day-care center is $10,000. Poor families pay $390 per year, middle-class families pay about $3,200, and the rich pay $5,300. When we lived in France, our son, Jeremy, attended a crèche in the Latin Quarter. The fee was $3,850 a year.

The staff of 19 was responsible for 72 children. The director, Odile Caplier, is a registered nurse who spent two years studying child development. Like all municipal crèche directors, she has an apartment in the same building, enabling her to keep a child past 7 P.M. in an emergency. The staff includes a deputy director (also a registered nurse) and two teachers (each with the equivalent of four years of college). The 12 child-care aides are high-school graduates who have taken a one-year course in child development.

What wowed my wife, Miriam, was the food. She often mailed copies of the crèche's weekly menu to friends in the United States so they could salivate over the poached fish, cauliflower mousse, parsleyed potatoes and Camembert cheese—not bad compared with the peanut butter sandwiches served at so many American preschools.

Concluding that our daughter, Emily, would do better in a more intimate situation, we sent her not to a day-care center but to a day-care *home*. France has 30,000 such homes—what amounts to a network of full-time government-licensed baby sitters who look after 57,000 children under the age of 3. Baby sitters must pass medical and psychological exams, and their homes are inspected for safety.

Once a month, Danièle Naudin, the matronly director of a municipal day-care center in western Paris, goes on her rounds. She pushes open the door of a turn-of-the-century brown brick building, walks up two flights of stairs and presses the doorbell of one of the eight baby sitters under her supervision.

"Bonjour, Mme. Naudin," Malika Akdim says, as she opens the door to her apartment, where she is looking after two girls, 11 months and 19 months old.

Naudin organizes monthly training sessions for the baby sitters, teaching them how to cope with emergencies, keep children clean and prepare healthful meals. One morning a week, the baby sitters take their charges to the center, where they play with other children and are examined by doctors.

Eager to encourage baby sitters to work within the system instead of in an off-the-books limbo, the French are trying to make the job more respectable and lucrative. Akdim, who emigrated from Morocco 15 years ago, has three school-age children and earns about $1,000 a month as a baby sitter. The local government provides bedding, bottles, toys and strollers for the children she cares for. The national Government has created an incentive for parents to use licensed sitters by refunding the Social Security taxes they pay (about $800 a year). . . .

France also offers parent-run day-care cooperatives and short-term drop-in programs. Municipalities put up money to build the cooperatives and provide a child development specialist to work with parents. Government-run "garderies," which are akin to indoor playgrounds, offer a few hours' respite for parents. Paris is experimenting with a center for children in "difficult" family situations that provides special care night and day supervised by a psychologist and social worker. Called Enfant Présent, it works with the court system and social service agencies.

Small wonder that many American educators and child-care experts—including Hillary Rodham Clinton—have looked to France as a model. Four years ago, as chairwoman of the Children's Defense Fund, she was one of 14 American experts who took part in a study of French child care sponsored by the French-American Foundation. "We found that most programs in France looked as good as the best American programs," says Gail Richardson, director of the foundation study. "What you see for everybody in France is what you see for just a small percentage of people in the United States."

French child care is not perfect, Richardson concedes. Though the ratio of children to teachers in French preschools, sometimes more than 25 to 1, is high by American standards, it is offset by the use of teachers' aides and by extensive teacher training. Most French preschool teachers have the equivalent of a master's degree. But don't expect the First Lady to make a big push for a French-style system anytime soon. The simple reason is cost.

Even if the White House were to unfurl a grand plan for child care, Federal, state and local governments would no doubt squabble over how to finance and control it. American and French taxpayers' attitudes toward spending on social services are very different. Almost half of France's gross domestic product goes to taxes, compared with less than a third in the United States. Even after the conservatives ousted the Socialists in the April elections, and amid signs of growing worry about France's budget deficit and high payroll taxes, the French are clamoring for more, not less, spending on child care.

In Paris over the last decade, crèche enrollment has doubled to 22,000. But in some neighborhoods, there still aren't enough places for all the children that need them. And in this year of deep recession throughout France, local officials say they are feeling intense pressure to hold down the cost to the taxpayer. The solution: continue building day-care centers while charging parents, especially the rich ones, more.

During the 70's, most middle-class and rich French parents preferred to use nannies. But attitudes changed radically after research demonstrated that socialization is important and that children who had been in crèches and écoles maternelles did better in the first years of elementary school.

"Nowadays, most parents want collective care, which is exactly the opposite of 20 years ago," says Sylvie Rayna, a researcher for the Ministry of National Education. "Now everybody seems to be demanding a place at a crèche."

❧ ❧ ❧

Questions

1. Explain how the French and American daycare systems differ.

2. What are "garderies"? What is their function?

3. Describe the problems with the French child-care system. Do these problems outweigh the benefits? Explain your answer.

4. Could a system like the one embraced by the French be put in place in the United States? Why or why not? How might implementing this system change family life?